Buddhism and Pali

Richard Gombrich

MUD
PIE

Mud Pie Books
43 Leckford Road, Oxford OX2 6HY
Registered Co. No. 4405635

ISBN 978-0-9934770-4-1

MUD
PIE

This book is dedicated to
Victoria Ying Jin
and
Yojana Bhagat
with admiration and
in gratitude for their support.

Na hi verena verāni sammantīdha kudācanaṃ.
averena ca sammanti; esa dhammo sanantano.

Never in this world is hatred pacified by hatred.
It is pacified by absence of hatred; this is the eternal law.

Dhammapada verse 5

Contents

Prologue: Discovering Pali 1

1 Pali in History 9
2 The Linguistic Character of Pali 25
3 Pali Prose Style 46
4 Pali in Buddhist Ideology 69

Epilogue: The Future of Pali 99

Notes 105
About the Author 109

Prologue

Discovering Pali

PALI IS THE name of a language which was born in ancient India and has mainly been used in a major Buddhist tradition, the Theravāda.[1] For many Buddhists, Pali occupies the kind of place that Arabic occupies for Muslims, Hebrew for Jews, Greek and/or Latin for various kinds of Christians. This means, naturally enough, that most people in the world have never even heard of Pali, let alone know anything about it. So how did I get to hear of Pali and find it worth devoting a large part of my life to studying and teaching it?

My father, Ernst Gombrich, was born in Vienna in 1909 and educated there. He moved to England in 1935–6. I am his only son, born in London in 1937. He was widely known as an art historian, but his interest in history was far wider than the fine arts, and in his passport he described himself simply as a historian. Much of his academic life was based at the Warburg Institute. This was a library founded in

Hamburg for the study of how, down the centuries, the ancient world (primarily Greece and Rome) has in all sorts of ways permeated our Western culture. The founder, Aby Warburg, was a member of the rich Warburg banking family. Because he was Jewish, when the National Socialist (Nazi) party rose to power it was decided to move his library to London, where it became the Warburg Institute, a part of the University of London. My father joined it as a very junior research fellow, held several positions there, and retired as its Director in 1972. While still a student in Vienna he published (in German) *A Short History of the World for Young Readers*. Its English translation is still in print.

The relevance of all this to me and to Pali is that I was deeply influenced by my father's dedication to cultural history. His chief interest in my education was that I should learn Greek and Latin; so I ended up attending St Paul's School in London, which was founded in 1509 by John Colet, Dean of St Paul's Cathedral and friend of the great humanist Erasmus, to educate boys 'from all nacions and countres indifferently'. This appealed to my father, who hated all forms of nationalism. At St Paul's I specialised in classics, and won a scholarship in that subject to Magdalen College, Oxford.

After 18 months at Oxford, I felt that I had had

more than enough of Latin and Greek, which in those days were still taught with a very narrow philological approach. As a university student, my father had studied some Chinese – and he always retained great enthusiasm for Chinese art and other facets of traditional Chinese culture. But, sensibly, I was put off the idea of switching to Chinese because in those Maoist days no foreigner could get a visa to study in China.

My best friend at school, Michael Coulson, had gone up to Oxford ahead of me; he had chosen to study Sanskrit and was enjoying it. Here was another great classical civilisation; my father had never studied it himself, and for me at the age of 22 that was an added attraction. So I followed in Michael's footsteps.

So have we reached Pali and Buddhism? Not quite. My father, an admirer of Voltaire, never in his life liked or admired any religion; but of course a cultural historian has to learn about that subject too. In his *Short History of the World*[2] he had a page on the Buddha – rather well done, I think – and though he had not taken his interest further, he considered the Buddha rather as a sage than as a promoter of irrationality. His library included a few volumes of German translation from the Pali Canon. I read a couple of books on Indian religion and was intrigued. In the year I left school, 1955, I read a new paperback by the American pragmatist philosopher E.A. Burtt, *The Teachings of the Compassionate Buddha.*[3] This book contains translated extracts from Buddhist scriptures, with comments by Burtt. I was much impressed.

In the same year, like most boys in my age group, I was drafted into the army for two years of 'national service'. Luckily there was no war on. I was posted to Germany, ending up in Hanover. My father was friends with the director of the Hanover Art Gallery, Gert von der Osten. He and his family were kind to me and I spent much of my free time at weekends with them. During the war, Frau von der Osten had converted to Buddhism. She brought up her two children as Theravāda Buddhists and held occasional meetings in her house; there were very few Buddhists in Germany at that time. I took part (my German was quite good) and also read a few pieces she gave me.

I would not say that I even came close to being converted, but I did become attracted by the Buddha's ideas, particularly the ethics and psychology – as I have been ever since. I suppose that like my father I was content to study religion as an 'outsider' and was interested in the religion's origins and history, so that like him I could, and do, call myself a historian. And from my father, and those around him, I understood that thorough and perceptive study of any culture requires intensive language study in the academic tradition with which I had been inculcated at school.

Back to Oxford, 1959–61. The syllabus for the BA in Sanskrit prescribed that one also study a 'minor' language: the choice was between Pali, Prakrit, and Old Persian with Avestan. The minor language was studied for 2 hours a week during the six eight-week terms of the course. I chose Pali, though Oxford employed no one to teach it. Nominally that became the duty of the only Sanskrit teacher, Professor Thomas Burrow. He was a comparative philologist with no interest at all in the content of the texts he taught as samples of language. So I was self-taught, and have learnt from experience that that is a poor way to study a language.

Not only did Oxford not provide teaching in Pali: Buddhism did not feature on any syllabus. It might have been taught to students of Chinese or Japanese, but it wasn't, and in those days Korean and Tibetan were not yet available as courses. It was possible to take a single paper on Buddhism in the final examination in Theology, but extremely few people did. To set me a paper in my final examination, the University had to invite an 'assessor', Dr Edward Conze, a learned but eccentric Anglo-German scholar. Apparently, no one thought it worthwhile to tell Dr

Conze what aspects of Buddhism I had studied, with the result that when I picked up the question paper I had a nasty surprise: of the dozen or so questions, there was only one on a topic I had even heard of. So I sat and wrote an answer to that one question for the entire three hours of the examination – and was no less surprised when I learnt that it had been given a first class mark.

I had a few wonderful teachers at school, and I greatly enjoyed and benefited from my years at Oxford, especially from my fellow students and the libraries, but I consider that the formal side of my Oxford education was appalling, and this opinion has led to the way in which my recent life has been involved with Pali. I was President and Treasurer of the Pali Text Society 1994–2002, and Co-Editor of its *Journal* 1996–2002, but this did not give me much scope for reform or innovation. When I took retirement (mandatory on becoming 67) from my Oxford Chair in 2004, the situation at Oxford for learning either Pali or Buddhism reverted to being almost the same as when I was an undergraduate in 1959–61: my post had been in Sanskrit, so there was no requirement for my successor to know or teach either of those two subjects. More by luck than judgment, I managed to exploit Japanese generosity and persuade the Numata Foundation (Bukkyo Dendo Kyokai) to endow a chair in Buddhist studies at Balliol College; but this still did nothing for Pali.

I therefore founded the Oxford Centre for Buddhist Studies (I paid for it, because I did not know anyone else who would) and used it as a vehicle for Buddhist studies in general but particularly for teaching Pali. Experience of my pupils had taught me (see Epilogue below) that a course of less than a hundred hours spread out over more than two years was an absurdly inefficient way of imparting a language; moreover, that the tradition (inherited from the pedagogy for Greek and Latin) of learning a classical language by translating *into* it from English literature was a perverse waste of time, since surely what motivated people to study Pali was wanting to find out what the texts said? I was also dissatisfied with the available language primers, which I found inaccurate and unintelligently composed. So I wrote my own primer, and devised an introductory course which aims only to enable pupils to *read* Pali texts after three weeks of intensive study. At the time of writing I have given this course or very similar ones about two dozen times to pupils from all over the world, and I believe that only a couple of students have not achieved the aim of the course. Nowadays I deliver the course live over the internet with two assistant teachers.

In giving the course, I also use it to put into

practice my theories about teaching and education, but to discuss these here would take me too far from Pali. For my discussions of the sad decline of Pali studies, I refer readers to my editorials in the *Journal of the Oxford Centre for Buddhist Studies.*

When Tony Morris told me of his proposal for a series of short books which explored some kind of connection (often remote) with Buddhism, and asked me to write one on 'Buddhism and Pali', I had mixed feelings. On the one hand I was sceptical about whether I could write a book about a little known language which would not be too dry to appeal to the general public. On the other hand, perhaps this was a rare opportunity to explain to the world why Pali mattered. If I succeeded, this could indeed persuade many more people to study Pali themselves.

Why would that be such a good thing? I began one of my books by writing that I consider the Buddha to be one of the greatest thinkers – and greatest personalities – of whom we have record in human history: 'I think that his ideas should form part of the education of every child, the world over, and that this would help to make the world a more civilized place, both gentler and more intelligent.'[4] And the best source for his ideas is the texts of the Pali Canon.

After summarising the history of Pali (Chapter 1), this book explains the main features of its grammar

(Chapter 2) and of its style as it appears in the Buddha's sermons (Chapter 3). The Canon's content is ascribed by tradition to the Buddha himself, and the question uppermost in the minds of many readers may well be how far to trust that ascription. As I explain at the beginning of Chapter 1, a recent book by two Buddhist monks argues for the unfashionable position that basically the ascription is correct. In Chapter 4 I go even further and argue that the Buddha was probably responsible not only for the content of much of the Canon, but even for the language in which it is expressed. Finally, the Epilogue considers how Pali can have a brighter future.

1

Pali in History

Introduction

Pali is the ancient Indian language in which the earliest Buddhist scriptures have been preserved, and remains the scriptural and liturgical language of the conservative branch of Buddhism known as Theravāda, 'the Doctrine of the Elders'. The scriptures are ascribed by Buddhist tradition to the Buddha himself. Is this claim plausible? Fortunately, in 2014 a book was written by two Theravāda monks, Bhikkhu Sujato and Bhikkhu Brahmali, which has precisely that focus. It is called *The Authenticity of the Early Buddhist Texts*, and it argues persuasively that the texts are far more authentic than it has been fashionable among modern scholars to allow. It has not been printed, but is available for free download on the website of the Oxford Centre for Buddhist Studies (OCBS), as a supplementary volume of the

OCBS Journal. It is written in an accessible style and gives references for everything that it says. In my opinion it is far and away the best thing ever written on this fascinating question, and everyone with an interest in the history of Buddhism should read it. Since it is easy to get hold of, I have tried in this book to resist the temptation to quote them on every topic, but hope that occasionally I have been able to offer a fresh perspective.

The name 'Pali' and its historical associations

MOST LANGUAGES ARE named after peoples who have used them and/or the geographical area where they have been used; but this is not the case with Pali. The word 'Pali' (which in Pali can also be spelled with a dot under the *l* : *Pāḷi*) is connected with a Sanskrit verbal root '*paṭh*', meaning 'recite', and originally meant 'text for recitation'.

The name 'Pali' originated as an abbreviation for *Pāli-bhāsā*,[5] which means 'the language (*bhāsā*) of the texts-for-recitation (*Pāli*)'. Those texts are collectively referred to as the *Tipiṭaka*, which literally means 'the set of three baskets', and Buddhists hold them to be 'the word of the Buddha' (*Buddha-vacana*). The

Tipiṭaka is usually referred to in English as 'the Pali Canon'. We know that the Pali Canon was composed orally. So can we be sure that the texts in it are literally the Buddha's words? The answer is controversial. We shall present the arguments later in this book.

The Buddha was born, lived and died (aged about 80) in north-eastern India. (In those days there was no boundary between what is now India and what is now Nepal.) He died very close to 400 BC. The earliest dated evidence for writing in India is inscriptions of edicts by the Emperor Asoka,[6] who ruled most of the Indian subcontinent c.269–c.231 BCE. (One edict mentions some texts from the Canon, though not in the Pali version.) So it seems unlikely that writing was used before the end of the fourth century BCE, which is to say fully a century after the Buddha's death.

At least until then the Pali texts were preserved by the monks and nuns who were his disciples, whose duty it was to memorise and recite them. Brahmins, the hereditary priestly caste, preserved their own sacred texts orally, in Vedic Sanskrit, starting from a much earlier date and in some cases until modern times, and we have ample evidence for their accuracy, so in this the Buddhists must have tried to emulate them. In both cases, brahminical and Buddhist, the chief concern was not to lose anything, but there was considerable editing and expansion.

This is important. When we argue that some texts go back to the Buddha himself, we are not thereby assuming that all of them do! The Buddha declared that all things created are impermanent; no sensible person can believe that the canonical Pali texts as preserved have undergone no changes at all in the course of their long history, and in this book we can take the fact of such changes for granted. This leaves a lot for scholars to argue about.

What kind of a language is Pali, in terms of its origins? This question requires two kinds of answers: the answer given by the Pali tradition itself, and the answer given by modern philologists. Within the Pali tradition, Pali used to be known as *Māgadhī*, i.e. the language of Magadha. Magadha was the ancient name for a part of north-eastern India: it had no precise boundaries, and referred at different times to an area of different extent, but Magadha may very approximately be equated with the modern state of Bihar. This name 'Bihar' is the word in both Pali and Sanskrit for a Buddhist monastery, and tells us how important Buddhism has been in that area. The capital of Bihar today is Patna, and that is the same city as Pāṭaliputra, which was the capital of the Mauryan Empire (late 4th to late 3rd century BCE). The third ruler of that empire, Asoka, by his patronage helped Buddhism to expand over most of India and even beyond. Since the Buddha spent his adult life in and near Magadha, Pali was named *Māgadhī* in the belief that it was the language that he spoke and therefore it must have been the language spoken around him.[7] The great exegete Buddhaghosa (5th century CE) wrote that if a child heard no other language it would grow up spontaneously to speak *Māgadhī* (our 'Pali') and that it was the root language[8] (from which, presumably, all other languages derive); but there is no evidence for such a belief in earlier sources. On the contrary, we know that the Buddha recognised the conventional nature of all languages, including his own.

Pali is by no means confined to the Pali Canon; it has continued to be used by Theravāda Buddhists. When Buddhism was established in places outside India (Sri Lanka being the first), they resorted to Pali just as the brahmins used Sanskrit. After that, the 'texts for recitation' came to be contrasted with other texts in the same language, particularly the commentaries on those same texts. The Pali tradition has a special word for commentary, *attha-kathā*,[9] which literally means 'telling the meaning'. (This is further discussed in Chapter 4.) Pali has also been used for other exegetical works, for chronicles, and in due course for other literary works, not all of them closely related to the early scriptures. Pali has also been used as a spoken language and a means of communication between learned Buddhists. However, one can safely say that with insignificant exceptions Pali has been used only by Theravāda Buddhists and that most texts written in Pali are closely linked to that religious tradition.

A brief history of the Pali language before the Canon was written down

We shall now look at the early history of the Pali language from a linguist's point of view.

Modern philologists classify Pali as a Middle Indo-Aryan (MIA) language; within the Indian tradition, this same group of languages is called Prakrit. Both these terms describe the languages directly derived from Sanskrit, which philologists also call Old Indo-Aryan.

The ancestry of Pali can be traced backwards as follows.

Step One: Old Indo-Aryan can be divided into classical Sanskrit, which was codified by the grammarian Pānini (probably 4th century BCE), and the preclassical language, Vedic Sanskrit. Scholars have agreed that Pali originated in the period between the end of Vedic Sanskrit and the beginning of classical Sanskrit, very approximately 5th to 2nd century BCE;

but if the theory proposed in Chapter 4 of this book is correct, we can date it more precisely to the Buddha's lifetime in the 5th century. (This period also saw the rise of what we call Epic Sanskrit, the language of the *Mahābhārata* and the *Rāmāyaṇa.*) Pali thus began as an early form of MIA, though it has some features which came about long after the Buddha's day; for example, some were inserted by Burmese grammarians in the 12th century.

Step Two: Sanskrit is a branch of Indo-Iranian.

Step Three: Indo-Iranian is a branch of Indo-European. Indo-European is the theoretical reconstruction by modern linguists of a language (with many dialects) which must have been spoken three and more thousand years ago by people who originated somewhere near the Black Sea and came to range over a wide area.[10]

Some readers may wonder how, then, Pali is related to English. Indo-European, of which no direct record survives, is the ancestor of many modern languages, from Sinhala and Bengali in the South and East to English and the Celtic languages in the Northwest, and also of many languages now dead. If we bear in mind that what we count as a generational step is rather arbitrary, since most linguistic change is gradual, we could say that both Pali and Anglo-Saxon, from which English is descended, are grandchildren of Indo-European. Therefore it is not absurd to say – though it must not be taken too literally – that English is a second cousin once removed of Pali.

There is a widespread popular misunderstanding to the effect that Sanskrit is the oldest Indo-European language. It is true that the evidence for Sanskrit is much older than that for most (not all) Indo-European languages; but that does not mean that the language itself is older than others for which the evidence is later. One must distinguish between two kinds of evidence: oral and written. It is plausibly argued that most of the oldest Sanskrit text, the *Ṛg veda*, goes back to the latter part of the 2nd millennium BCE (greater precision is not possible); but it was not written down for well over a thousand years. As mentioned above, the earliest dated evidence for writing in India, Asoka's inscriptions, is from the middle of the 3rd century BCE. Writing was probably used in the far northwest of India (modern Pakistan/Afghanistan) at a somewhat earlier date, in a script which soon died out and left no descendants, but for the general cultural history of India that is marginal. Asoka's inscriptions were in forms of Middle Indo-Aryan, not in Sanskrit. There is good reason to think that texts in both Sanskrit and Middle Indo-Aryan began to be written down in the

2nd century BCE or slightly earlier, though no direct evidence for a written text (as against an inscription) of that period survives.

This distinction between the types of evidence available is essential to clear thinking about the history of Pali. Let us work backwards through time. Most of the physical evidence for Pali is surprisingly recent: the bulk of the Pali manuscripts surviving in Sri Lanka and Burma/Myanmar were copied in the 18th and 19th centuries. Many manuscripts in northern Thailand, recently brought to wider notice by Oskar von Hinüber, date from the 16th century; only a handful of manuscripts known from elsewhere are older than that. The grammarians who systematised Pali grammar and prosody in Burma in the 12th century exercised considerable influence on how the language was written thereafter in Burma, and thence to some extent elsewhere.[11] However, analysis of the only Pali manuscript to antedate those grammarians shows a language identical in most respects to that preserved by the later manuscripts. This oldest witness consists of four leaves of a manuscript of a canonical text; it is in Kathmandu and dated on palaeographic grounds to c.800 CE. It seems to have been copied from a north Indian original some centuries older.[12]

Whether we consider the Kathmandu manuscript

the oldest substantial piece of written Pali to survive is to some extent a matter of definition. There are older seals with Pali formulae, just a few words long, inscribed on them. There are also two inscriptions, found in India and dated to the 5th century CE or close to it, which have several lines of canonical text; they are in a dialect of Middle Indo-Aryan very close to the Pali we know from other sources, but with some phonetic differences, so that Prof. von Hinüber calls them 'continental Pali'.[13]

According to the Theravāda chronicles, the Pali Canon was first committed to writing at a monastery in central Sri Lanka in the 1st century BCE, during the reign of Vaṭṭagāminī Abhaya.[14] The act of writing down the text must have stabilised the content of the Canon, even though whether or not a few specific texts are to be considered canonical (i.e. part of the Tipiṭaka) has not been settled to this day.

Writing down a text does not ensure its perfect transmission any longer than that original copy is preserved; every time a text is copied out, errors occur. The commentaries on the Canon, most of which are ascribed to Buddhaghosa, though he mainly edited older material, record quite a few variant readings and pass over other textual corruptions (as they are apparent to us) in silence. Nevertheless, those corruptions affect only a tiny proportion of the total text; they are far too limited to obscure our view of the character of its language as a whole. That language we may safely assume to have been Pali, very much as we know it and as it is described in today's grammars.

How, then, does this Pali, the language in which the Tipiṭaka was consigned to writing, relate to the language in which the Buddha preached? Modern scholarship has assumed that the two cannot be identical, but that Pali must have originated in some specific part of India at some date, neither of which correspond to the time and place of the Buddha's lifetime.

In recent years the range of opinion has narrowed, so that everyone who does not feel constrained to accept the orthodox Theravādin account has been accepting the following:

We know that the Buddha spoke a form (or several forms, as he travelled) of MIA; that he lived in the 5th century BCE,[15] so that the Sanskrit to which his speech was most closely related was pre-classical;[16] that he explicitly permitted his followers to translate what he had said (in conscious contrast to the *Ṛg veda*, of which the very sounds were sacrosanct); and that the texts into which his words came to be formalised were preserved orally by the monks and nuns for many generations. It is also evident that just as there is a gap in time of nearly 400 years between the death of the Buddha and the writing down of the Pali Canon, there is a distance of some 1,500 miles between the area in which the Buddha lived and central Sri Lanka. As Buddhism and its texts grew older and spread geographically, the dialects used must have changed and proliferated. Before the texts were written down, it is not likely that that the differences between the dialects were clearly conceptualised; it must have been a matter of reciting in what appeared like 'regional accents'.

To all the above, many would add: Pali was formed at the phonetic level by the spelling conventions which the first scribes chose to adopt. The Pali sound system contains inconsistencies many or most of which must be due to spelling conventions. During these early centuries of Buddhism, brahmins were exhaustively discussing and categorising the Sanskrit sound system; it was in terms of the sound values of Sanskrit that MIA dialects could be formalised and thought about. All the early (i.e. BCE) Buddhist texts were in forms of MIA; and when they came to be written down, as we can see not only in the case of Pali but also in what is called Buddhist Hybrid Sanskrit, there was a tendency to move words towards their Sanskrit spellings. Indeed, this was a recurrent tendency in the history of Pali. This is easy to understand if we think of an analogy: when a modern novelist or playwright wants to record the speech of characters who use an English dialect, she does not provide a full phonetic transcription of that dialect speech – which hardly any readers could follow – but compromises with the spellings of standard English.

While the previous two paragraphs would have the assent of most modern scholars, I consider that it leaves unsolved certain problems about how the Pali texts originated, and by coming at the question from another angle I have been able to propose a new solution, which I present in the last chapter of this book.

Pali in the last thousand years

So much for the first half of its history. What has happened to Pali since then?

The Theravāda Buddhist tradition, Pali's social vehicle, was virtually confined, so far as we know, to Sri Lanka and south-east India for over a thousand years. In the 11th century it spread to Burma and thence, during the next three centuries, to much of the rest of continental South-east Asia. In each country Pali was somewhat influenced by the main language in use in its surroundings. Thus, for example, the Pali written in Sri Lanka and on the adjacent mainland of India shows traces of Sinhalese and Dravidian influence. In Cambodia (where the first Pali is in an inscription dated 1308–9) local influence went so far that there developed a macaronic language, a mixture of Pali and Khmer[17] (not treated in this book); but that seems to have been exceptional.

The main influence on the development of Pali, however, continued to be Sanskrit. Again and again in its history – the inscriptions and the Kathmandu manuscript mentioned above furnish examples – there is a tendency to drift back to Sanskrit spellings, or at least to Sanskrit phonetics. What does this distinction mean? Again, let us take an English parallel. Some English dialects (e.g. Cockney) lose initial *h*. A scribe anxious to correct Cockney may restore standard English phonetics by supplying an initial *h*, but he may not be restoring English spelling if he puts an initial *h* where it does not belong: 'I ham happy to see you'. The Burmese grammarians of the 12th century, for example, performed analogous feats with Pali.

Buddhaghosa, especially in his great compendium of Theravāda doctrine, the *Visuddhi-magga* ('The Path to Purity'), wrote a Pali which was influenced by classical Sanskrit in syntax and style. After the scholarship of the Burmese grammarians, works came to be written in a Pali which was virtually calqued on Sanskrit: the distinctive morphology of Pali and its earlier vocabulary were preserved, but any Sanskrit lexical item could be turned into Pali by mechanically applying phonetic rules, and Sanskrit sentences could similarly be transposed into Pali without paying much attention to the distinctive features of earlier Pali idiom and style. In this sense the use of Pali, even though it could serve as a medium of communication between monks who had different mother tongues, became highly artificial.

Lexicographers have tended to ignore this latest phase of Pali, and that is not unreasonable since in theory any item in the Sanskrit lexicon could be represented in Pali without changing its meaning. For the practical purpose of describing the language, then, the development of Pali is generally considered to end with the Burmese grammarians. Thus we can summarise by saying that Pali has undergone changes and development over the centuries: least in morphology (grammatical inflection) but quite noticeably in phonetics, syntax, style and vocabulary. As Oskar von Hinüber has put it, Pali is not so much a 'dead' language as an artificial language that has been repeatedly reshaped.[18]

2

The Linguistic Character of Pali

Introduction

For many years I have been teaching courses in Pali, under the auspices of the Oxford Centre for Buddhist Studies, to people from virtually all over the world. The aim of those courses is to enable people working by themselves with dictionaries to read canonical Pali prose. The main course is introductory, and I have written a primer of the language to serve as its backbone. Much of the information in this chapter can also be found in that course book, but naturally it goes into far more detail. A reader who finds the basic information in this chapter too dry should skip it but try not to miss the passages on more general topics concerning the language.

Basic linguistic features

PALI IS DERIVED from Sanskrit. It is related to Sanskrit much as Italian is related to Latin. Speaking quite loosely, it is reasonable to describe Italian as a simplified Latin, and Pali as a simplified Sanskrit. For historical reasons, in the modern world, both in the West and in India, the pedagogic tradition is that Sanskrit should be taught first, and this is how Pali is always taught in universities; only in monasteries and a few other Buddhist institutions is Pali taught without constant reference to Sanskrit. This has greatly impeded the spread of knowledge of Pali.

Let us glance at the four areas into which analysis of a language is commonly divided: phonology, morphology, syntax, lexicon.

Phonology deals with the system of sounds used by a language. Pali has simplified the Sanskrit sound system and lacks several of the letters/sounds of Sanskrit.

Morphology deals with word formation, the main feature of grammar. Here Pali has simplified Sanskrit even more drastically. To give but one example: Sanskrit has three (grammatical) numbers: singular, dual and plural; Pali has eliminated the dual and has only singular and plural.

Syntax concerns how words are arranged to form more complex units; here Pali mainly follows Sanskrit rules but there are differences in idiom.

The great majority of words in the Pali lexicon are derived from Sanskrit, with the appropriate phonetic changes, but many of them undergo some changes in meaning as well as in sound. Grammarians long ago worked out how the phonetics of Sanskrit words changes when they are used in Pali, so by applying those changes the vast majority of Sanskrit words can be introduced into Pali – even though this makes the resultant Pali sound artificial and moves it away from its canonical form.

The pronunciation of Pali varies between the countries where Theravāda Buddhism is traditional, because it has been affected by the phonology of the local language. However, there is a consensus among experts that the pronunciation in use in Sri Lanka preserves an authentic tradition, in that it is quite plausible that Buddhism (in its Theravāda from) was imported from the Indian mainland round the middle of the 3rd century BCE. In ancient India the phonetics of Sanskrit was studied with care, since Sanskrit mantras (prayers and spells) were thought to be effective only if they were perfectly pronounced. Though the Buddha did not subscribe to such a view, the Indian cultural tradition evidently influenced its near neighbour, so that the pronunciation of Pali sounds reflected those of their parallels in Sanskrit. The one exception, concerning the letters *e* and *o*, will be explained below.

Before describing the Pali sound system, we must explain how the language is written. Pali is a language, not a script. There is no such thing as a Pali script; Pali can be written in any script. In the West it has almost always been written in the Roman script, which is clear and unambiguous if to the normal alphabet one adds some diacritical marks. Along with the use of the Roman script goes a small set of conventions in punctuation. Unlike in, say, Indian manuscripts, we separate words by spaces, take advantage of the clarity added by using capital letters for proper names, and make use of such punctuation as full stops, question marks and quotation marks.

Writing Pali in the Roman script often involves using two signs to convey a single Pali sound.

Firstly, two Roman letters may convey one Pali sound. This happens in English too: examples are *ch* and *ee* in 'cheese', *th* in 'the', *ck* in 'back'. All the Pali examples of this kind involve writing an *h* after another consonant. This does not have the same effect on pronunciation as in English: it always means that the preceding consonant is aspirated, i.e. immediately followed by an *h* sound. Thus Pali *kh* is pronounced like the *ckh* in 'backhand'; Pali *gh* is pronounced like the *gh* in 'doghouse' and so on. Therefore in pronouncing an unaspirated Pali letter, such as *k* or *g*, one must take care not to aspirate it at all. In spoken English slight aspiration occurs very often and is rarely noticed. Remember, the aspirated and unaspirated versions are different letters in Pali.

Secondly, some letters are written with diacritics, i.e. signs which differentiate letters. The diacritics with which most English speakers are familiar are the French accents over certain vowels, e.g. crème brûlée. In Pali some vowels have a bar over them; this is the diacritic called a macron and means that that vowel is long: *ā, ī, ū*. Some consonants too have diacritics. Again, remember that the diacritic makes the letter it is applied to into a different letter – not just some kind of variant form. In other words, to mix up, say, *a* with *ā* is just as bad a mistake as to mix up *a* with *o* or *i*.

Just as the English language does not have a set of aspirated stops, it does not have the set of consonants *ṭ, ṭh, ḍ, ḍh, ṇ and ḷ*, which in Pali are referred to as cerebrals or retroflex, and which are written with a dot under them. These are pronounced with the tip of the tongue curled back against the hard palate. By contrast, for the dental stops (which are written with no dot) the tongue is against the teeth, and may even slightly protrude beyond them, as in French or Italian. English *t* and *d* thus fall between the cerebrals and dentals of Pali. In theory, the same applies to *ṇ/n* as to the two kinds of *t* and *d*, but in practice the distinction between *ṇ* and *n* is often hard (or impossible?) to hear. The same goes for the rare letter *ḷ*, whether aspirated or unaspirated. Neither *ṇ* nor *ḷ* ever stands first in a word.

With only three exceptions (for which see below), a Pali letter is always pronounced in the same way. As for a general guide to pronunciation, although Pali is full of aspirates and Italian has none, in most respects the pronunciation of Pali and of Italian are quite close. There are no silent letters in Pali: for example, a double consonant is always pronounced distinctly; thus *vata* is pronounced with a clear difference from *vatta*.

Obviously in order to use a Pali dictionary one has to accustom oneself to an alphabetical order completely different from that in the Latin tradition, but this task is made easier if one follows the rationale of the sequence. The sequence of the letters in the alphabet follows the Sanskrit tradition, which reflects a sophisticated analysis of how the sounds are articulated. The vowels precede the consonants, and in each set of consonants the sequence is from the back of the mouth to the front.

A strange feature of the Pali alphabet (as of the Sanskrit one) is that one of the sounds of the language is neither a vowel nor a consonant, and is not listed in the alphabet because it cannot stand alone as a separate letter. It is named *anusvāra* (or sometimes *niggahīta*); it is most commonly written as *ṃ* (an *m* with a dot under it); and it can only follow a short vowel. It is pronounced through the nose, like English *ng* with no separate *g* sound at the end.

Syllabification, scansion and stress

This small section is of the utmost importance: anyone who wants to understand how Pali works, or to get a feel for how it sounds, must give it top priority.

(1) The vowels in Pali, in alphabetical order, are *a*, *ā*, *i*, *ī*, *u*, *ū*, *e*, *o*.

The bar over a vowel is (in English) called a macron, and indicates that it is long. If there is no bar over the vowel, this means that it is short. (As will be explained in para 6 below, this does not however apply to *e* and *o*.) A vowel with a macron is a different letter from one without, just as in Pali *k*, for example, is a different letter from *kh* (see above).

(2) A syllable of a Pali word is a part which ends in a vowel, whether or not the vowel is nasalised.

Thus the word *upasaṃkamāmi* ('I approach') has six syllables: *u pa saṃ ka mā mi.*

(3) In Pali every syllable is either long or short. (In India the terms are 'heavy' and 'light'.) It is essential both to know which is which and to make the difference clear in pronunciation.

(4) A syllable is long for one of three reasons:

(a) It contains a long vowel. A long vowel makes a syllable long, but a syllable can also be long for one of the other two reasons.

(b) Its vowel is followed by *ṃ* (*anusvāra*).

(c) Its vowel is followed by more than one consonant.

(5) *A syllable cannot be long for more than one reason.* There are very few exceptions to this rule and they are almost all in words loaned from Sanskrit. This rule means that a long vowel can never be followed by *ṃ* or by a conjunct consonant. If word formation threatens to make this happen, either the vowel is shortened or what follows the long vowel is changed.

(6) By themselves, *e* and *o* are long. If they are followed by *ṃ* or by a conjunct consonant, they become short. What is confusing is that no system for writing Pali (so far as I know) marks whether an *e* or *o* is long or short. However, there is no ambiguity in the pronunciation.

(7) The *stress* in a Pali word falls on the penultimate syllable if that is long. If it is short, the stress goes back (towards the beginning of the word) until it finds a long syllable. (For purposes of stress, however, detachable parts like verbal prefixes do not always count as part of a word, so that occasionally one has to understand a word in order to know where the stress falls. Examples: kamánti 'they go', kámati 'he goes', upasaṃkámati 'he goes' – the stress here goes no further back because upa and saṃ are verbal prefixes.)

Most English speakers have a strong tendency to stress words on the penultimate syllable, so that they mispronounce some Indian words, for example Himālaya, Bhagavato.

(8) There is one case in which stress affects another aspect of pronunciation. The vowel *a* (short *a*) has two different pronunciations. In a stressed syllable, and in the first syllable of a word, it is open like the *u* in English *but*. Otherwise it is the middle vowel, like the last sound in English *butter.*

(9) A Pali word cannot end in a consonant; but a beginner looking at a Pali text may think she is seeing some exceptions to this. These exceptions are in circumstances inherited from Sanskrit: two words are felt and pronounced as one, because the second is very weakly pronounced; the consonant in

question is thus felt to be medial, not final. Example: *tad api* 'that too'. In such a case the two words may be written as one: *tadapi*. The whole is stressed as if it were a single word, which means that the first word (here *tad*) carries the stress and the second word (here *api*) carries no stress at all.

(10) The material in this section is also essential for the appreciation of Pali verse. Its main feature is not rhyme but using set patterns of words arranged either by number of syllables, or by quantity (i.e. whether syllables are long or short), or both. More detail will be given in a separate section below. The same kind of patterning also plays a role very occasionally in prose.

Sandhi

Anyone who has poked their nose into Sanskrit will be aware that the language has a feature called *sandhi*, 'junction'. It occurs in many other languages too, but in Sanskrit it is so prominent that the term has been adopted in linguistics to label it wherever it occurs. It refers to the fact that the phonetics of a word is affected by the phonetics of the word that follows it, and sometimes *vice versa*. Little *sandhi* is recorded in written English; but when one says 'bed 'n' breakfast' both the beginning and the end of the word 'and' have been affected by *sandhi*. In the Cockney 'gotcha', the *tch* is *sandhi* for the *ty* in 'got you'.

The rules of *sandhi* in Sanskrit are very complicated but rigidly adhered to. The situation in Pali is quite different. The commonest situation is that between two adjacent words in a sentence *sandhi* is not applied at all. Sometimes, however, the Sanskrit *sandhi* is preserved, particularly within a short phrase such as *tad eva*; the pure Pali would be *taṃ eva*, but the *tad* is inherited from Sanskrit. *Sandhi* within a compound (*samāsa*) is common, particularly to avoid a hiatus between vowels: thus *kāma-aggi* would tend to become *kāmaggi*. Since *a+a* normally gives *ā*, and indeed this word in Sanskrit would be *kāmāgni*, what has happened here to the *a*? The answer is given in the previous section above: a double consonant cannot be preceded by a long vowel in a Pali word, and this applies to every word, even if that word is a *samāsa*.

Occasionally the *sandhi* in Pali prose, particularly when it involves very short words, is bewildering. But it is extremely rare that *sandhi* impedes understanding. Where one may need to know a bit more about *sandhi* is in verse; that will be explained in the section on prosody below.

Syntax and sentences

When one learns about language, one initially assumes that meaning is conveyed by words, but one soon realises that single words convey little unless they occur in a context. It is not possible to formulate a general rule about the size or structure of the linguistic unit which does most to convey meaning, but generally it is reasonable to say that meaning is conveyed in sentences.

The topic of how words in a sentence relate to one another is called syntax. How the words are related is mainly determined by two features: word order and morphology – changes made to the word to show its grammatical function. In English both are used but word order is far the more important.

Let us examine the sentence: 'The hungry boy sees the black cows.' The word order tells us (1) that it is the boy who is hungry, not the cows; (2) that it is the cows which are black, not the boy; and (3) that the boy is seeing the cows, not vice versa. In Pali the same would be true for (1) and (2), because there is a general rule – even more widely applicable than it is in English – that a word precedes the thing it describes. In Pali 'sees', the verb (the 'doing' word), tends to come last.

The great majority of changes to words which

reveal their grammar is lacking in modern English. Nevertheless, the final *s* of 'cows' tells us that there is more than one cow, while the lack of such a final *s* tells us that there is only one 'boy'. The great majority of nouns can form a plural by adding an *s*. As for 'sees', the final *s* tells us that the subject is singular, not plural, whereas if the word were 'see' we would take it to be a plural.

In most Pali prose sentences both word order and inflection guide us to the meaning. In verse, however, words commonly have to be arranged to meet the demands of the metre, so one depends more on the inflections to convey the meaning. Quite a few inflections are ambiguous, and this means that verse is less easy to understand, or at least to understand rapidly, than prose.

Another feature of Pali is its fondness for the passive. The English sentences 'I have read the book' and 'The monk speaks these words' are likely to appear in Pali as 'The book has been read by me' and 'These words are spoken by the monk.' English stylists tend to condemn such uses of the passive as what used to be called 'officialese', the language of bureaucrats, but in Pali they contribute to elegance. One of the inflections of any noun is called 'the instrumental case' and is used to denote the agent of a transitive verb in the passive; and there is a strong tendency for that agent to stand first, or at least very early, in the sentence. Because of the fondness for the passive, that means that in the first of my examples 'by me' will stand first, or at least very early, in the Pali sentence, and the same goes for 'by the monk' in the second example.

Like Sanskrit and other related languages, Pali has a kind of verb we call a causative. This can be formed on the basis of almost any simple verb. Thus from 'to be' there is a verb 'to cause to be', from 'to die' a verb 'to cause to die', i.e. to kill. This usage lends precision to descriptions of events in a hierarchic society: a king does not build a palace but causes it to be built, a landowner does not plough a field but causes it to be ploughed (or, in neater English, 'has it ploughed').

Of all the features of Pali syntax, perhaps the most pervasive is the use of nominal compounds (in Pali: *samāsa*). This is both common and intricate, and when learning Pali one must pay serious attention to it. I find it shocking that Geiger's *Pali Grammar*[19] does not mention this topic at all, and to my mind most primers pay it far too little attention. The only European language which has anything at all like it is German: as in Pali, German compound nouns can contain a very large (in theory infinite) number of members.

My exposition of compounds owes a great deal

to the work of Michael Coulson, who during my teens was my best friend at school, remained a close friend later at Oxford University, taught Sanskrit at Edinburgh University and wrote the book *Teach Yourself Sanskrit.*[20] Unfortunately he died before it was published and it fell to me to see the book through the press. His analysis closely follows the classical Indian grammarians, and he was clever in illustrating it with English examples.

A common kind of compound which is not very common in English is called 'exocentric' because it refers to something outside itself. A 'redcoat' is not a type of coat but a man with a red coat (in olden days, a soldier); in the phrase 'two-car family', 'two-car' is being used as an adjective qualifying 'family'. English uses it in insults: an 'egghead' is a person with an egglike head, not just the head of such a person. Many of the names of Buddhist monastics are exocentric compounds. For example, the words *dhamma* ('the Buddha's teaching') and *sāmi* ('master') combine in the monk's name Dhammasāmi. This does not mean 'Master of/in the teaching' but 'Having the teaching as his master'.

Verse

In Pali, verse is defined by its use of metre not rhyme.

There is far more prose in the Pali Canon than verse. An individual text is not necessarily entirely in prose or entirely in verse. Quite a few prose *sutta*s contain some verse. Texts which are essentially poems often have brief prose introductions.

A special case is the *Jātaka*, the huge collection of stories about the Buddha's former births. There were originally 550, but three have been lost. The kernel of each story is in verse, and the whole collection is arranged by the number of verses: stories containing only one verse come first, and the last story in the book, the *Vessantara Jātaka*,[21] has 786 verses. Scholars can see that the verses are very old and their text is often corrupt. The prose, which is of later date, narrates the story in full. Clearly the custom was for people with a particular interest in teaching or learning the *Jātaka*s to memorise the verses, which were considered canonical and therefore sacrosanct, and to recompose the prose each time the story was told. Technically the prose is called the commentary, using the same term for 'commentary' (*atthakathā*) as that used for the commentaries on *sutta*s and other parts of the Canon. This literary form, in which the crucial part is in verse and the rest is repeatedly recomposed in prose around it, occurs in quite a few contexts in the literature of Sanskrit and other Indian languages.

The description I have just given of the *Jātaka* book is only very approximate, but we do not have the evidence which would allow us to be more accurate. As it stands, each section begins with an 'account of the present' (*paccuppanna-vatthu*), which explains the occasion when something occurs in the Buddha's life which reminds him of an episode in one of his previous lives. His recounting of this episode is then the *Jātaka* story itself, called the 'account of the past' (*atīta-vatthu*); it includes the verses, the first words of which serve as a kind of title for the story. To the verses is appended what we nowadays call a 'word commentary', which gives the kind of explanations of grammatical and other detail in the verses which we would normally expect of a commentary. Though one would assume this 'word-commentary' to be a separate final stratum, in fact it is sometimes mixed up with the narrative prose. At the end of the narrative the Buddha briefly gives a key or 'application' (*samodhāna*), identifying the main figures in the story as former lives of figures 'now', i.e. present in his lifetime.

Prosody: the use of long and short syllables

Many metres are used in Pali. Some of them count

syllables, others count quantity, using the principle that one long syllable equals two short syllables. However, things are not quite that simple. In a metre based on counting syllables, there are rules in the standard pattern that certain syllables should be long or short; this imitates or inherits the situation in Sanskrit.

As is the case in Sanskrit too, almost all the metres used in Pali are considered to consist of units – we might think of them as verses – of four lines, which are in fact called quarters (*pāda*). In some metres, the pattern of each quarter is the same; in others, the first and third quarter are the same, and so are the second and fourth. The end of each quarter is supposed to coincide with the end of a word, though occasionally that word is within a *samāsa*. *Sandhi* applies between the first and second *pāda*s and likewise between the third and fourth. There should be no *sandhi* fusion between a vowel at the end of one *pāda* and a vowel at the beginning of the next. The gap between the second and third *pāda*s is felt to be greater than the gaps at the ends of the first and third lines.

One metrical rule which is universal is that whatever the length of the syllable taken in isolation, the last syllable of a *pāda* counts as long; it is as if the slight pause which will come in recitation at the end of a *pāda* is metrically a part of that last syllable.

A phenomenon in Pali versification which is hardly ever found in Sanskrit and considerably complicates matters, is that two short syllables may stand where there should be one long one, or a single long syllable may stand where there should be two short ones. The main reason for this is to be found in Pali's relationship to Sanskrit. Sanskrit *ārya*, for example, is normally *ariya* in Pali, but if it is metrically convenient the Sanskrit phonetics can be restored and *ārya* used.

An even more common kind of flexibility is that the normal (prose) form of a word can be tinkered with in certain standard ways. At the end of a word, the quantity of the final vowel, especially *i*, can be changed. Often a Sanskrit double consonant, as in *appiya*, can be single in Pali, giving *apiya*. Probably the commonest license of all is to play around with *anusvāra*. In some positions, particularly at the end of a word, an *anusvāra* can be omitted, or an extra one inserted.

Here is an example:

In the phrase *dānaṃ passati* ('He sees a donation') the second syllable of *dānaṃ* is long, whether or not one takes the option of turning the final *anusvāra* into an *m* by *sandhi*. If one wants a short syllable in that position one writes *dāna*: there is a hypothesis that the omitted *anusvāra* leaves a trace of nasalization, but this cannot be proved or disproved. If on the other hand the phrase is *dānaṃ icchati* ('He wants a donation'), if one wants that second syllable to be long one again leaves the *anusvāra*, as would be normal in prose; but if one wants that syllable to be short, one applies *sandhi* and thus turns the *anusvāra* into the consonant *m*.

Some of the composers of Pali verse apparently were not very skilful, or maybe they preferred not to follow the metre strictly if doing so made the meaning less clear. Whatever the reason, those scholars who try to purge a text of corruptions can often not rely on metrical regularity as a guideline. Philologists who work on Sanskrit, Greek or Latin texts and try to establish the most likely readings find that a text in verse offers them an advantage in that the metrical rules are rather rigid, so that at least they can tell in advance whether a given syllable should be long or short. Of course this is sometimes true in Pali as well, but by no means always. On the other hand, if we have a text in Pali and also a version of that text in Sanskrit, the change of language will inevitably have effects of a metrical kind: the Sanskrit version of a Pali word may upset the metre, or the vocabulary may need to be changed if it is to fit in. In this case the metre is a fairly reliable guide to the direction of change.

Nowhere in the literature is it stated that the

Buddha himself composed poetry; but it seems very likely that he did. Probably the single most famous book in the Canon is the *Dhammapada, Words of Teaching*. This consists of 423 verses; most of them stand alone, but there are some pairs. The Sanskrit version of this text is called the *Udānavarga*, and the kind of changes mentioned in the previous paragraph make it certain that the Pali version is the older. This is not to say that the *Dhammapada* was originally composed in exactly the language in which we have it now, but it cannot have been very different.

The verses of the *Dhammapada* are ascribed *en masse* to the Buddha. The commentary on the text always describes on what occasion the Buddha uttered the verse(s), but it is a very late composition, maybe a thousand years after the time of the Buddha, so this information may not be reliable.

3

Pali Prose Style

Introduction

It is not always easy to draw sharp distinctions between style, idiom and grammar. But since I am writing mainly for readers who do not know Pali, I shall only attempt to deal with matters of style. The Pali Canon is one of the world's greatest documents of oral literature, and the greatest single factor in determining its style must have been that orality. So at this point we must introduce the still contentious questions of how it was created and how it was preserved. This will gradually lead us to consider in the following chapter the bold hypothesis that the Buddha may have been responsible not only for the content of much of the Pali Canon, but even for the language in which it is expressed.

The origin of the texts

THE 'THREE BASKETS' which constitute the Pali Canon contain (1) the *Vinaya*, which lays down the personal and communal rules by which monks and nuns should live; (2) the *Suttas*, mainly sermons in which the Buddha, or occasionally a leading monk, preaches (often to monks and/or nuns) the *Dhamma*, which deals with morality, meditation and ideas on matters which concern everyone; and (3) the *Abhidhamma*, a systematisation of the *Dhamma*, particularly its more abstract parts. When were these texts composed, and do we have anything like the original compositions?

Buddhist tradition holds that the texts of the sermons were formulated at the meeting which the monks held about three months after the Buddha's death. This meeting is known in English as 'the First Council', but the term translated as 'council' really means 'communal recitation'. The *suttas* were first recited, in response to questioning, by Ānanda, the monk who had been the Buddha's personal attendant during the latter half of his forty-five year preaching career. The *Vinaya* was similarly recited by the monk Upāli, who as an ex-barber had had the task of shaving ordinands and thus had presumably been present at all the early ordination ceremonies. Most versions of the tradition admit that the *Abhidhamma Piṭaka* must postdate this Council. When Upāli and Ānanda had formulated the texts, they were rehearsed by all the monks present (we hear nothing about nuns), thus beginning the tradition of the Canon's oral preservation.

The texts which were recited at the First Council must have had some kind of existence before that. There is an episode recorded in the Canon[22] in which the Buddha asks a young monk whom he is meeting for the first time to tell him some *Dhamma*; the monk recites a set of verses, the whole of a section of the *Sutta-nipāta* called the *Aṭṭhaka-vagga*, and the Buddha commends him. The text does not say who originally composed those verses; it could have been the Buddha himself; it could have been the young monk's teacher, Mahākaccāna, who was a reputed preacher; it could have been yet other monks; and it could have been a combination of these, since not all the poems need be by the same author. But it is clear that this set of sixteen poems was collected in the Buddha's lifetime and arranged on a principle followed both in the *Ṛg veda* and in many other parts of the Pali Canon, namely by increasing length.

The number of sermons preserved in the Pali Canon is very large: Theravāda Buddhists count them as 17,505,[23] a greater number than appears to have come down to us. Most of them are short, and the corpus is inflated by repetitions and redundancies. Even so, it is a massive body of literature, most of it in prose. Either at the outset or very early on the sermons were was divided into four collections, and monks and nuns specialised in learning by heart one of those four collections or another comparably large chunk of the Canon.

Memorisation

At this point it is necessary to dispel the scepticism likely to be found in the modern reader: can a fairly large group of young men and women be found, generation after generation (moreover, individuals who have not been selected for their exceptional mnemonic powers), who are capable of learning by heart such a lot of textual material and preserving it in their memories until the time comes to pass it on to the next generation?

Even as I was preparing to write this chapter, relevant evidence was published on the internet in a report from the *Scientific American.*[24] This report concerns controlled experiments conducted on professionally trained pandits in India. 'India's Vedic Sanskrit pandits train for years to orally memorize and exactly recite 3,000-year old oral texts ranging from 40,000 to over 100,000 words.' The brains of the trained pandits and those of controls (matched brahmins not so trained) were scanned by magnetic resonance imaging (MRI), and 'numerous regions in the brains of the pandits were dramatically larger than those of controls, with over 10 per cent more grey matter across both cerebral hemispheres, and substantial increases in cortical thickness.' The most striking effects were found in parts of the right cortex associated with 'precise sound pattern encoding and reproduction.' Moreover, though it is not clear whether this aspect of memorization was the focus of experiments, the author's own experience of studying Sanskrit orally was that he acquired the 'ability to exactly repeat lecturers' own sentences when asking them questions in class', and others told him of having experienced the same effect in themselves.

At the time of the Buddha, the brahmins had already for centuries been preserving their sacred literature, the Vedic texts, orally. We shall explain below how in many respects the Pali Canon is modelled on Vedic literature. The brahmins had already divided into schools (called 'branches') which specialised in particular texts. Learning the texts by heart was virtually coterminous with their education; and that education could last for up to thirty-six years. The Buddhist Saṅgha must have operated in a very similar manner. And the similarities did not stop there. Long after the invention of writing, the Brahmins were reluctant to write down Vedic texts and continued to preserve them orally. In their case this was motivated, at least in part, by a wish to keep them away from people not entitled to know them: women and people of low caste. Though lacking that motivation, Buddhists seem to have done the same: they relied more on memory than on written texts, which they rarely consulted – as I observed was still the case in Buddhist villages in Sri Lanka when I did fieldwork there in my youth.

Modern scholars have collected Vedic texts orally preserved hundreds, even thousands, of miles apart in India. There are some variants, but astonishingly few, given that the tradition is between two and a half and three millennia old. Therefore the research results of James Hartzell (see footnote 24) come as no surprise. Moreover, the Vedic oral tradition aimed to preserve texts verbatim, not to recompose them as time went by, so it is likely that Buddhists did the same.

We have so far been discussing the preservation of what was recited at the First Council. But what happened before that? How did the sermons originally take shape, before they were recited by Ānanda?

Some readers may think that I have already taken speculation far enough: we have no written record of any kind from those days, so can we probe any further with our questions? Some of us, myself included, are prepared to accept that the Buddha gave a sermon of which, years later, Ānanda gave a version at the First Council, and that those present then set to work to ensure that others memorised it and it was given a place in the accepted collection of the Buddha's teachings. But people seem not to ask how the sermon got from the Buddha to Ānanda, and from Ānanda to the communal tradition, without the use of writing, let alone any more modern recording device.

It is here that I find the Hartzell research fascinating. There can be only one answer to the question I have just posed, and it is the same answer for both questions: *memory*. Ānanda must have developed an excellent memory for what the Buddha preached, and when he reproduced it all at the First Council the senior monks could replicate the feat. The logic of the situation suggests that their achievement was a bit less difficult than Ānanda's, because they could help each other out. Many of the Buddha's sermons were addressed to groups of monks, so they could no doubt help Ānanda to recall what the Buddha had said, but he presumably was a virtuoso. In our times we know of individuals who have photographic memories: they just have to see a page of a text and they can then carry it in their heads and read it at their leisure. In those days there was no place for such mental photography, but a parallel aural feat must have been known to exist and could be cultivated. Nowadays it would probably only be relevant in the world of musical performance, where there are many professional musicians on record who have memorised whole scores.

In the Pali Canon the word *bahussuta* is commonly applied to an individual, and usually translated into English as 'learned'. Literally, however, it means 'who has heard a lot'. Thus having heard a text was conventionally equated to knowing it.

To anyone who remains sceptical I can only say, how else could the Vedas or the Pali Canon have been preserved?

Pali prose is characterised by a lot of repetition and other forms of redundancy. It is often argued that this is because it records what the Buddha said – his sermons – and as a skilful preacher he provided a good deal of redundancy to make his message more easily memorable. My own account of how the text of the Buddha's First Sermon originated runs: 'It was delivered to five disciples who became the first five monks after the Buddha himself. No doubt some or all of the six people present on that occasion remembered what the Buddha talked about. This probably blended in memory with what he "should" have talked about in order to introduce others to the insight he had had ...'[25] So I present the text we have as a reconstruction. That may work for a very short and simple text delivered to a tiny audience like the First Sermon; but since we have to posit true memorisation as a crucial feature of ancient Indian religious and cultural traditions, why not assume it in the case of the First Sermon as well?

The style of canonical Pali prose

There is a matter of style which is actually laid down in the work of Pāṇini,[26] the ultimate authority on Sanskrit grammar. Pali prose is rich in strings of two or more words which are grammatically parallel; often we might want to call the longer ones 'lists'. Pāṇini lays down that words in strings are ordered by increasing length. Length is here defined by the number of syllables. This rule applies even when the relevant words are in a nominal compound (*samāsa*). A further refinement is that when two words have the same number of syllables, a short syllable is less than a long one – as is true in metrics – and therefore comes first; however, this refinement is not very strictly adhered to. Immediately below I discuss another stylistic topic concerning strings of words and illustrate it with a string of four words starting with *sandiṭṭhika*. The first two of them have four syllables and the latter two have five, keeping to the rule of ascending length.

The next feature of this style to be discussed is much more important, because it affects meaning. In this case the words in the string are not only grammatically parallel but are also close to synonyms, with some overlap in their semantic range. (The example given below will make this clearer.) This technique can, and often does, convey to the perceptive recipient a multi-faceted meaning. Thus each word in the string appears in the dictionary to have a range of possible meanings, some obviously closely linked and some less so (or sometimes not linked at all). To find the meaning most appropriate to the context we look for one which coincides, exactly or approximately, with a meaning of the previous word, and we adopt the hypothesis that that pair of meanings, one in each of the two words which are next to each other, applies in this context. Sometimes there is nothing more to it, so we may even have a case of pure redundancy. But often the words also have other meanings which may fit the context, and we add to our hypothesis that those other meanings are also part of the intended message, further implications. We apply this method of interpretation to all the words in the string.

Before I make this abstract explanation clearer by giving an extended example of its working, it may help some readers if I compare it with a feature of Western classical music. There may be a succession of chords, each of which repeats all the notes of the previous chord except one, for which it substitutes a new note. When we hear the whole sequence of chords, our mind has a different appreciation of each of them from what it would get if each chord were just heard in isolation. The effect of hearing all of them in close sequence conveys something richer and more complex than if we heard them separately – which is of course why the composer has constructed the music in that way.

There is a standard description of the Buddha's teaching, the *Dhamma*, which is so common in the Canon that it has come to be used as a liturgical formula. While the stylistic feature which we particularly wish to describe applies most clearly to the string of four words starting with *sandiṭṭhiko*, it also has a bearing on the rest of the formula, so we shall look at the whole of it.

Svākhāto Bhagavatā Dhammo
sandiṭṭhiko akāliko ehipassiko opanayiko
paccattaṃ veditabbo viññūhī ti.

The first line means: 'The Teaching has been well spoken by the Blessed One.' Both *Dhamma* and *Bhagavant* (I use the stem form, which is how we refer to such words) are technical terms and as such cannot of course be translated at all, but *Bhagavant* refers to the Buddha and *Dhamma* to what he taught. Some people translate *Dhamma* 'truth', and that cannot be called wrong, if the truth and what the Buddha taught are held to be identical. The defect of 'truth' as a translation is that *Dhamma* not only includes true statements but also valid injunctions: 'ought' as well as 'is'.

Svākhāto is a nominal compound *(samāsa)* of two words: *su* and *ākhāta* (which can also be spelled *ākkhāta.*). *Su* means 'well' and *ākhāta* (a past passive participle in the stem form) means 'spoken' or 'told'. By a rule in Pali phonetics, *su* before a vowel becomes *sv*, but the pronunciation hardly changes.

Saying that the Buddha's teaching is 'well told' has a particular resonance. The *Ṛg veda*, the most ancient brahminical text, is a collection of hymns, and each hymn is called a *sūkta* . This word derives from *su-ukta*, 'well spoken'. The phonetic change from Sanskrit to

Pali means that in Pali *sūkta* becomes *sutta*. In the Pali Canon, the majority of the prose texts, nearly all of which report the Buddha's words, are called *sutta*. On top of that, one book of the Canon is called the *Sutta-nipāta*. *Nipāta* means 'collection', so this title means 'Collection of *suttas*'. In this case each *sutta* is a poem, in verse, so that the similarity to the brahminical use of the word is even closer. The commentarial tradition does not point out that naming a text '*sutta*' must be a reference to brahminism, and hence a competitive claim, but this silence is probably not significant, as that tradition rarely points out when the Buddha is alluding to brahminism unless he does so explicitly.

This use of the concept 'well spoken' had a post-Canonical history as well. At first it was said: 'All that it spoken by the Buddha is well spoken.' Later this was turned round and became 'All that is well spoken has been spoken by the Buddha.' This could be maintained only when it had been accepted that the Buddha was (or, rather, all Buddhas were) omniscient.

The fact that the Buddha is here referred to in the third person need not indicate that these words were composed by someone else. Unless he is talking of a time before his Enlightenment, the Buddha in the Canon normally refers to himself in the third person.

We turn now to the string of four adjectives which qualify the Buddha's teaching. Here I follow the convention of the lexicographers: a comma between meanings indicates that they are roughly synonymous, while a semi-colon indicates that what follows may be regarded as a distinctly different usage. I am using the *Pali-English Dictionary* by Rhys Davids and Stede[27] (in fact mostly by Stede, because Rhys Davids died early in the enterprise) and *A Pāli Dictionary* by Margaret Cone,[28] which only goes up to words beginning with *n*. Both are published by the Pali Text Society.

sandiṭṭhiko. PED: 'visible; belonging to, of advantage to, this life; actual.' The verbal root in this word means 'to see'. There exists a noun *sandiṭṭhi*; *sandiṭṭhiko* is an adjective built on it. It means 'the visible world, worldly gain'. So *sandiṭṭhiko* is most likely to mean 'connected to the visible world', or 'to worldy gain', which can of course be any kind of gain. When we compare this word to the three that follow, we shall see that this is best summed up in English by the word 'practical'.

akāliko. Kāla means 'time'. This is a possessive adjective in the negative. PED: '1.not delayed, immediate, in this world, combined with *sandiṭṭhika*; 2.subject to time, i.e. temporal, vanishing; 3.unusual, out of season.' Cone: '1.not dependent on time; not limited to a particular time; immediate, immediately effective; 2.not at a usual or expected time; unseasonable.'

The references given under 2 and 3 by the PED and under 2 by Cone suggest that these meanings are late (probably post-canonical). Part 2 of the PED entry is rather puzzling, as 'subject to time' seems to contradict Cone's 'not limited to a particular time'. We note that 'not limited to a particular time' suggests English 'timeless', and bear that in mind as a possible additional meaning. However, the primary meaning which looks likely to go best with *sandiṭṭhika* is 'immediately effective'.

ehipassiko is refreshingly unambiguous. It is built with the same suffix, *-ka*, on two imperatives: *ehi* 'come!' and *passa* 'see!'. There is no rule in Sanskrit grammar which allows such a compound: it is obviously an idiom, the cry of a salesman offering something which you can see for yourself to be a good buy – a situation referred to again in the final line of the formula. So the *Dhamma* is 'a thing to come and see'.

opanayiko, the fourth adjective, is based on the verb *upaneti* 'lead towards'. PED's entry is brief: 'leading to (Nibbāna)'. Cone, more cautious, is much longer: 'fit for bringing near, for taking to oneself; fit for making use of; deserving to be used'. While PED's entry is attractively high-minded, Cone's ignoring this meaning must be intentional. The pattern of what precedes convinces me that the primary meaning intended is 'fit for making use of' – which again I would summarise, and translate as 'useful'. Other possible translations might be 'relevant' or 'applicable'. I expect that PED's interpretation derives from the commentarial tradition, and is a plausible additional meaning or implication.

paccattaṃ veditabbo viññūhi can be seen as a summary, just as the first line can be seen as an introduction. *Veditabbo* comes from the verb *vedeti* and is a kind of verbal adjective called a gerundive. Most gerundives contain an ambiguity, for they can mean 'to be X-ed', a mild obligation, or 'X-able', a statement of potential. *Vedeti* means 'know, understand', the agent is *viññū* 'intelligent', and *paccattaṃ* is an adverb meaning 'individually, by/for themselves'. So the whole phrase means that the *Dhamma* is to be understood *and* can be understood by intelligent people for themselves. This fits neatly with *ehipassiko*, but is also relevant to the other three adjectives. Here I have chosen to keep both possible meanings of the gerundive, because surely both meanings are intended.

I believe that anyone who has managed to follow my exegesis of this one short formula from start to finish will never again doubt that to become fully aware of the richness of the Buddha's meaning it is necessary to read his words in their original language. Nor is this the kind of language which is amenable to skim reading!

Repetition

The most obtrusive feature of canonical Pali prose is repetition. As we have said above, this feature of the texts is due to their being oral literature: what is repeated is less likely to be forgotten. This repetition is tedious and inconvenient for the modern reader, so much so that it seems plausible to argue that it acts as a deterrent. The manuscripts, and the printed editions that follow them, do make some attempt to reduce the amount of repetition by using a syllable (usually either *pe* or *la*) equivalent to 'ditto' in English; this however appears with very little consistency, which suggests that it is used with reluctance. When I once suggested to the Ven. Dr Walpola Rahula, a great Pali scholar, that it would be sensible to print the Canon in a far shorter form by using such abbreviations wherever possible, he was firmly against the idea; he said that very often in the series of repetitions there were small changes which abbreviators tended to overlook. This is certainly an important caveat, and I suppose it might be a good compromise to reserve abbreviated texts and the translations closely based upon them for certain purposes, warning users of the danger.

There can be very few *sutta*s which contain no repetitions, and there is little to be said about them; however, one can just point out that three kinds of repetition are particularly common.[29]

(1) Certain passages are repeated in *sutta* after *sutta*. For example, the beginnings of *sutta*s are heavily stereotyped. Many begin: 'Thus have I heard. On one occasion the Blessed One was living at Sāvatthi in Jeta's Grove, Anāthapiṇḍika's Park. There he addressed the bhikkhus thus: "Bhikkhus." – "Venerable sir," they replied. The Blessed One said this.' The proper names in this quotation are extremely frequent, but others are also common and do not create any change in the rest of the paragraph.

(2) The formula which typically concludes a *sutta* is briefer: 'That is what the Blessed One said. The venerable X was (or: the bhikkhus were) satisfied and delighted in the Blessed One's words.'

(3) More important is the repetition of the same wording to convey the same subject matter. We can call such passages set pieces, or borrow a term from biblical scholarship and call them pericopes. Pericopes vary in length from a few words to several pages, and a great many *sutta*s consist largely of

piling up pericopes. Some pericopes are particularly typical of one of the Nikāyas.

For example, in the *Majjhima Nikāya* the Enlightenment of a monk is often described thus:

> Before long, dwelling alone, withdrawn, diligent, ardent, and resolute, the venerable X, by realising for himself with direct knowledge, here and now entered upon and abided in that supreme goal of the holy life for the sake of which clansmen rightly go forth from the home life into homelessness. He directly knew: 'Birth is destroyed, the holy life has been lived, what had to be done has been done, there is no more coming to any state of being.' And the venerable X became one of the arahants.[30]

Another kind of repetition, closely related to the pericope, takes the form that something is said about several items. In English it would be natural to bunch these six items together at the beginning or end of the passage or both, and say what is to be said just once, referring to them as a list or group. Here, by contrast, is the Buddha talking about the five constituents of a living being, which Bhikkhus Ñāṇamoḷi and Bodhi translate as material form, feeling, perception, formations and consciousness.

'Bhikkhus, what do you think? Is material form permanent or impermanent?' – 'Impermanent, venerable sir.' – 'Is what is impermanent suffering or happiness?' – 'Suffering, venerable sir.' – 'Is what is impermanent, suffering, and subject to change, fit to be regarded thus: "This is mine, this I am, this is my self"?' – 'No, venerable sir.'

'Bhikkhus, what do you think? Is feeling ... Is perception ... Are formations ... Is consciousness permanent or impermanent?' – 'Impermanent, venerable sir.' – 'Is what is impermanent suffering or happiness?' – 'Suffering, venerable sir.' – 'Is what is impermanent, suffering, and subject to change, fit to be regarded thus: "This is mine, this I am, this is my self"?' – 'No, venerable sir.'

'Therefore, bhikkhus, any kind of material form whatever, whether past, future, or present, internal or external, gross or subtle, inferior or superior, far or near, all material form should be seen as it actually is with proper wisdom thus: "This is not mine, this I am not, this is not my self." Any kind of feeling whatever ... Any kind of perception whatever ... Any kind of formations whatever ... Any kind of consciousness whatever, whether past, future, or present, internal or external, gross or subtle, inferior or superior, far or near, all consciousness should be seen as it actually is with proper wisdom thus: "This is not mine, this I am not, this is not my self."'"[31]

Another common form of repetition is when

someone says something, and it is repeated, both by others and by the original speaker, as it passes from person to person. This sequence usually leads up to a more substantial speech by the Buddha, which contains the main message of the *sutta*. For example, the *Alagaddūpama sutta, sutta* 22 of the *Majjhima Nikāya*, begins as follows:

(1) A monk called Ariṭṭha has a bad idea which seriously misrepresents the Buddha's teaching.
(2) Several monks hear that Ariṭṭha has had this idea, which is repeated word for word.
(3) They go and ask him if he has had this idea, which is repeated word for word.
(4) He says yes, repeating it word for word.
(4b) They press him to drop the idea, mentioning things the Buddha has said which contradict the idea.
(5) Nevertheless, he sticks to the idea and repeats it.
(6) So the monks go to the Buddha and repeat everything so far, which means that the idea has now been stated ten times in all.

So the Buddha asks the monks to fetch Ariṭṭha, which they do. Then the Buddha asks Ariṭṭha if he has had this idea, and he says yes, thus repeating (3) and (4) above. At this, (6b) the Buddha repeats the things he has said which contradict the idea, as in (4b) above.

The Buddha tells Ariṭṭha that by misrepesenting his teaching he is slandering him and will become notorious. He then cross-examines the monks and gets them to repeat the things he has said which contradict Ariṭṭha's idea, and he then finally repeats those things himself.

Thus, by my calculation, Ariṭṭha's bad idea is repeated word for word 12 times, and the things the Buddha has said which contradict that idea occur 4 times.

The bad idea in question is that there is nothing wrong with a monk's having sexual intercourse, and the Buddha's remarks which contradict this are ten ways in which he has compared sexual intercourse to something which brings little satisfaction but much suffering, and impedes spiritual progress. So it is a very important message, which does need to be drummed in.

There is good reason to believe that this use of repetition goes back to the Buddha himself.

> If repetition was a conscious device used by later redactors to ensure fidelity, but not part of the Buddha's style, we would expect to find repetition only in those aspects of the texts that the redactors controlled. For example, we would find the same Sutta repeated in multiple collections.

> However, what we actually find is that repetition is prevalent at every level of the texts, whether the word, the phrase, the sentence, the paragraph, the passage, or the whole discourse. Repetition, like the other mnemonic features of the texts, is a characteristic of their composition, a characteristic that was further developed by the redactors. Since the early Buddhist texts were composed in the oral tradition, the mnemonic characteristics of the texts originated in the historical Buddha's teaching style.[32]

We shall return to this theme in the next chapter.

4

Pali in Buddhist Ideology

Introduction

The use of Pali lies at the heart of Buddhist ideology, in that when the Buddha was preaching and the Canon was being formed, it was conceived of as the opposite of Sanskrit, and thus symbolised a far-reaching rejection of Vedic brahmanism. In my view – perhaps shared by no other modern scholar – it may also have been the language that the Buddha spoke, at least when preaching.

The Sanskrit context

IN HIS LONG ESSAY 'Axialism and Empire',[33] Sheldon Pollock has eloquently expressed the relevant aspect of the Buddha's radical disagreement with Vedic/brahminical culture. He writes: 'It is in complete harmony with his[34] causal analysis of the human predicament that the Buddha and his disciples developed a wide-ranging understanding of contingency or conventionalism in human life, in opposition to the naturalism of the *vaidika* thought-world.'[35] By 'naturalism' Pollock here means that how things are is embedded in nature, and not the result of human activity. He then writes:

> Against the Mīmāṃsā[36] tenet that the relationship between word and meaning is *autpattika*, 'originary' or natural – a primal, necessary, and non-arbitrary relationship (sometimes absurdly reduced by its opponents to a mechanical, even magical view of reference) – Buddhists typically argued for a relationship based on pure convention ... What was at stake for Mīmāṃsā in asserting the uncreated, eternal nature of language is the possibility that *vāṅmaya*, or a thing-made-of-language – that is, a text, like the Veda – could be eternal too, something the Buddhists sought fundamentally to reject. About the fact that nothing in language generally or in Sanskrit particularly is transcendent, Buddhist doctrine is unambiguous. ... [T]he subversive inversion of *vaidika* terminology ... must

have resonated scandalously in the minds of twice-born candidates for membership: 'All mental formations' (*sarve saṃskārāḥ, sabbe saṃkhārā*) – in fact, all things formed, no doubt including all Vedic rites (*saṃskāra*) and perhaps even Sanskrit itself (*saṃskṛta*) 'are non-eternal'; they arise, and having arisen, disappear. It was again fully in keeping with such a theory of language that the early Buddhists rejected the use of Sanskrit, the language of the gods, whether in favour of local dialect or Pali, a new hieratic competitor language.

The creation of a Pali canon seems to have been a response to the presence of organized Vedic text-corpora. In its very structure, it embodies a range of Vedic architectonic principles, such as the arranging of texts in increasing segments, in the same way as we have seen it appropriate the genre title of *sūkta* (*sutta*).[37]

There are stark and instructive differences as well, however, that conform with other aims. The Vedic corpus increasingly sought to escape confinement in any spatiotemporal framework, and fully articulated this desire in the doctrine of the uncreatedness of the Vedic texts ... : Vedic texts are *apauruṣeya*, produced by no author human or divine, and existing outside of all history whether cosmic or terrestrial. Buddhist holy texts, on

> the other hand, typically specify the place, time, audience, and of course speaker – the Buddha – thereby enmeshing the very truth of the message in its concrete historicity.[38]

I find this passage by Pollock well worth quoting at length, but there is a great deal more to the matter than this. Before going further into this, however, I must make it perfectly clear that there is no evidence of the Buddha positively recommending Pali in the precise sense of the language which has acquired that name: he is simply deploring the use of Sanskrit. What he recommends is using the local language (or languages) derived from Sanskrit, what we now would call forms of Middle Indo-Aryan; in effect he is saying 'Use anything but Sanskrit'. However, I shall now go on to make a far more specific and radical suggestion.

Pali: the Buddha's answer to Sanskrit?

There is a famous passage in the Canon[39] which quotes the Buddha giving his view on which language to use. Unfortunately the terms he uses are not entirely unambiguous to us, so the passage has been dissected and discussed in far too many learned articles. I have given my detailed argument for their precise interpretation in my book *What the Buddha Thought.*[40] I conclude that when he was forbidding his followers to use *chandas*, he was referring to Vedic Sanskrit; and when he was saying that while studying his words they should do so using their own mode of expression, he was referring to explanatory glosses and paraphrases in their own dialects.

Since there is no writing in India dating from the Buddha's lifetime, how exactly the texts which constitute the Pali canon were originally formulated and in what language or dialect has to some extent to be a matter of conjecture, but the *Araṇavibhaṅga Sutta*[41] provides some helpful information. In it the Buddha gives a series of pieces of advice on how to avoid conflict by being moderate – often, indeed, by taking a middle way. He says that in various places people use a range of different terms for a dish or bowl. However, one should not insist on particular terms, claiming that they alone are correct and rejecting terms which are more widely understood.

In the previous chapter, I argued that it makes good sense to believe – as most traditional Buddhists do – that large parts of the Pali Canon do preserve for us the *Buddha-vacana*, 'the Buddha's words', transmitted to us via his disciple Ānanda and the First Council. In doing so I am following the work of Bhikkhus Sujato and Brahmali, mentioned at the beginning of chapter 1, though I have not been able to fit into my brief account all of their arguments for their position. To those arguments, however, I have added a demonstration that there is no reason to be sceptical about the capacity to memorise, which a conservative account logically requires.

In treating this topic, I have allowed it to appear that I am talking only about the *content* of what was transmitted, not about its language. But some readers may have wondered whether the two are entirely separable. I agree with them.

In what language, then, did the Buddha preach? Scholars have argued long and vehemently about this question. They start, as it were, from the other end: that we know that for several centuries after the Buddha's lifetime the canonical material was preserved in various forms of Middle Indo-Aryan. Initially this happened only by oral transmission and we shall never be able to retrace all the details of how these versions evolved; on the other hand, it is widely accepted that (as we set out in chapter 1) Pali is the form of Middle-Indo-Aryan used in first writing down the (whole) Theravada Buddhist Canon, which happened in Sri Lanka in the 1st century BCE.

Note two things about this. One is that it leaves wide open the possibility that at least some of the Canon was written down earlier, in Pali or some other form(s) of Middle Indo-Aryan. The other is that it does not claim that during transmission from the First Council until the 1st century BCE, the text had undergone no changes. While Sujato and Brahmali show that changes were mostly minor, other scholars, notably the Ven. Analayo, have recently shown that significant changes were made in the Pali Canon: for example, changes both of omission and of commission served to downplay the roles of the early nuns and change the story of how their Saṅgha came to be founded. Such changes must have been made with intent (in this case misogynistic);[42] others no doubt came about by accident.

The more we learn about the early history of the Buddhist canonical texts, the more fascinating it becomes, but also the more it becomes evident that we shall never be able to get a full and coherent picture of their evolution for the first half millennium or so.

So let us go back to the very beginning, i.e. to the Buddha himself, and try to see if we can thus make better sense of the story.

Because of various inconsistencies, such as the use of some Sanskritisms and borrowings from other dialects, it is often said (I have said so myself) that Pali is an artificial language. But what does this mean? Modern English evolved from a large admixture of Norman French into Anglo-Saxon, and we still frequently add gallicisms and other borrowings from foreign languages, just as they adopt English words and expressions. More to the point: even the language of the *Ṛg veda* is not genetically pure: it includes features of different ages and vocabulary from non-Indo-Aryan languages. Its language is called Sanskrit, ‘composed’, and that composing has included many forms of innovation.

Language, dialect, argot

Indeed, what exactly is a language, as distinct from a dialect? It has been said that a language is a dialect with an army. This clever adage refers to a language which is the daily medium of communication, a mother tongue, not to a sacred language preserved for use in specific contexts. In the case of India, those who study its languages have reported that if one walks across northern India from east to west or *vice versa*, one observes that the local spoken language changes gradually in small steps. Starting from the west, from the coast of the Arabian Sea in Gujarat, one can keep going east in a fairly straight line and pass through Madhya Pradesh, Bihar and then into Bengal, reaching the eastern coast on the Bay of Bengal; in this case one encounters only three officially named languages: Gujarati, Hindi (the state language of both Madhya Pradesh and Bihar) and Bengali. If one takes a slightly more southerly route, one goes through Maharashtra (state language: Marathi), and after Madhya Pradesh goes to Bengal via Orissa (state language: Oriya). Or, taking a more northerly route, one goes through Rajasthan (language: Hindi), another move north takes one to the Panjab (language: Panjabi), then through Hariyana and Uttar Pradesh (state language of both: Hindi again), then Bihar, and finally Bengal. All these named languages are closely related, and as one goes by any of these routes the language gradually changes from Gujarati to Hindi to Bengali. Locally some of the dialects have their own names; this is particularly true of Hindi, which covers the widest area. The decision to say that at a certain point on the map the name of the language has changed is mainly determined by politics – power relations both past and present. However, to the ear of the traveller on the ground all that appears is a gradual shift in dialect. (It is also politics which will determine which script is used.)

Once officialdom has recognised a language, but probably not before then, it is decided which forms are 'correct' in a language and which deviant, or 'incorrect'. This formulation of what is correct can happen at all linguistic levels: phonology, morphology, syntax, lexicon; but it is probably most clearcut at the morphological level. In English, for example, there are rather few permitted variants in morphology: 'sheeps' as the plural of 'sheep' is incorrect in standard English, whereas 'fishes' is a permitted plural of 'fish', but the two forms 'fishes' and 'fish' differ in usage. The creation of a set of rules laying down what is 'correct' can occur only when the language has a written form, though once the rules exist they can be, and often are, applied to the spoken language as well. To put this the other way round: where there is no writing, the language in daily use has no official, standard form: no dialect has superior authority.

The Buddha was continuously travelling through a large area of north-eastern India, and as he moved from village to village he had to communicate in a range of dialects. So presumably he had to work out for his own use something which would serve as a kind of *lingua franca*. The fact that Pali is a little closer to Sanskrit than are the other forms of Middle Indo-Aryan would be the natural outcome of this situation. It could also have developed as years went by and the early Buddhists were trying to make their texts intelligible in a wider geographical area.

It is uncontroversial that Pali includes Magadhisms

which probably reflect how the Buddha spoke, at least initially, when he first attracted followers. In the Prakrit of Magadha (as we know from early inscriptions) a final *o* in case endings was changed into an *e*. The commonest Pali word for 'monk' was *bhikkhu* and in the general pattern of Pali phonetics its nominative and vocative plural was *bhikkhavo*. But throughout the Canon, when the Buddha addresses monks ('O monks!') he says *bhikkhave*. So this is likely to be a 'frozen' form, a reminiscence of how he spoke. If one example is felt not to suffice, let me cite a word from the very first line of the first sermon: *sukhallika*. The context shows that it means much the same as the shorter word *sukha* 'pleasure'. Modern scholars call the *–allika* suffix a Magadhism. The word is found only here (though the entire phrase in which it occurs is repeated in a couple of late texts). So this looks like an accurate memory of how the Buddha sounded when he began to preach to his monks.

While I think this point about Magadhisms is probably uncontroversial among modern scholars, I propose to take it much further.

Pali has some strange irregularities. It has a few common Sanskrit loan words like *brāhmaṇa*; this has to be considered a loan word because it breaks two general rules of Pali phonetics: that a word cannot begin with a double consonant; and that before a double consonant inside a word any vowel has to be short. One can see that this particular word is borrowed from Sanskrit because its meaning is inextricably associated with Sanskrit; and yet it is odd that other words closely associated with the culture of Brahmins undergo the normal phonetic changes. An even more striking feature is Pali's use of alternative forms. For example, the commonest word for 'there' can be either *tattha* or *tatra*. The latter is the same as in Sanskrit, while the change *tr* > *tth* is rare, though found in some other pronominal words. To me it seems that far the most likely explanation for this variation is that *tattha* and *tatra* come from different dialects. This phenomenon is multiplied in the morphology. Thus the commonest of the noun declensions, masculine and neuter stems which end in *-a*, have three options (*dhammā*, *dhammasmā*, *dhammamhā*) in the ablative singular and three (*dhamme*, *dhammasmiṃ*, *dhammamhi*) in the locative singular. In verbs the optative is similarly threefold: for example, the first person singular is *bhave*, *bhaveyyaṃ* or *bhaveyyāmi*. This range of variants in morphology is surely exceptional among languages.[43] I could draw up a list, but that would be unreadable, and those who know no Pali would find it uninformative, while those who do know it can draw up the list for themselves by leafing through the standard grammars.

I attribute this remarkable variety to dialect variation, in the sense that Pali includes material, especially optional forms, from various dialects. Modern scholars have labelled some of the variant forms 'vedicisms' or 'archaisms'. It is true that some of them reflect older forms of Sanskrit than the Sanskrit contemporary with the Buddha, but this does not tell against my argument, because archaisms are found in dialects all over the world. I do not deny that sometimes a Vedic form may have been used, particularly in verse, to give an archaic effect; but that will only account for a small minority of cases.

Though bold, my hypothesis can be made more convincing by further considering specifics both of geography and of the social use of language. Much of this specificity must be credited to Dr Alexander Wynne, to whom I showed much of what I have written above soon after writing it.

When Pali is systematically compared to Sanskrit, its phonetics look more western than Magadhi. Our earliest evidence for dialect geography is the inscriptions of Asoka, which are widely scattered across India (mainly its northern half), and on that basis we can confidently say that Pali has a preponderance of what, two centuries (or a bit less) after the Buddha, were western rather than eastern features. The evidence for where the Buddha preached is provided, as Pollock reminds us, by the preambles to the texts of the sermons.

On reading my first draft, Alex Wynne sent me an e-mail. I must introduce it by explaining that the Buddha was born in Kapilavatthu, now over the Indian border in Nepal; that he spent time in Rājagaha (modern Rajgir), which is also where the First Buddhist Council was held soon after his death; and that the largest number of his sermons seem to have been delivered in Sāvatthi, which was then capital of the kingdom of Kosala, situated c.100 miles north-east of modern Lucknow.[44] Wynne wrote:

> Since Kosala was the major power in the Buddha's lifetime, since Kapilavatthu was absorbed into Kosala even then, and since the Buddha spent most of his time in its capital Sāvatthī, the basis of his dialect would probably have been Kosalī, not Māgadhī, and Sāvatthī is as close to Delhi as it is to Rājagaha – so it would surely have had a 'Western' type dialect.

He continues: 'In chapter 9 (p.153) of his *Buddhist India*, T.W. Rhys Davids defines the language of Kosala as follows: "A conversational dialect, based probably on the local dialect of Sāvatthi, the capital of Kosala, and in general use among Kosala officials, among merchants, and among the more cultured classes, not only throughout the Kosala dominions, but east and west from Delhi to Patna, and north and south from Sāvatthi to Avanti".' Wynne summarises: 'Pali as the basic language of Buddhism is based on Kosalī, which the Buddha and his followers expanded by including many more local and archaic forms, particularly Easternisms/Māgadhisms, as they wandered over a wider geographical area.'

Rhys Davids published *Buddhist India* in 1903.[45] It has taken us a long time to catch up!

Dr Imre Bangha, University Lecturer in Hindi at Oxford, has sent me an e-mail in which he offers further support to my argument:

> [T]he modern three-language formula (cosmopolitan English, lingua franca Hindi and the local language) may have been in use already at the time of the Buddha as cosmopolitan Sanskrit, lingua franca Kosali/Pali and local dialects ... The lingua franca was useful in towns with populations in contact with mobile people while the dialects must have been maintained by farmers. The lingua franca, due to its closeness to the dialects and to its composite nature, may have been passively understood by most speakers of dialects.

There is perhaps one way in which the Rhys Davids and Wynne formulation can be slightly improved on. When Rhys Davids calls the language of Kosala a 'conversational dialect … among the more cultured classes' he is expanding our understanding of dialect to specify not only geography but also social class. The word 'argot' is used nowadays to refer to 'the jargon or slang of a particular group or class'.[46] In traditional societies it may refer to a form of language specific to a certain cultural group, for example, thieves or butchers. It is reasonable to suppose that in ancient India members of a particular religious movement were also initiated into a particular argot with its own idiom and terminology. If so, Pali presumably represents the argot of the Buddha and his earliest followers, and was preserved within their community down the centuries. This would explain how it could come about that in the time of Asoka the mission that brought Buddhism to Sri Lanka brought it in the language of the Pali Canon.

My theory, then, is that Pali reflects the idiosyncratic language used by the Buddha as he toured northeast India and communicated with a population ranging from brahmins to untouchables. When after some years his followers wrote down what he said and made some attempt to standardise it by giving it a set grammar and an orthography, they were to some extent guided by the only grammar and orthography which existed in their culture, those of Sanskrit, but they were also concerned to retain as best they could the precise characteristics of their teacher's language as preserved by their oral tradition.

Thus, just as the Buddhists modelled their canon (and many features of its contents) on the Vedic canon which was the lifeblood of Vedic culture, they also did so by retaining the language that their teacher had created for them as an analogue to Sanskrit. The extent of its use in the first few centuries we shall never know, but as Buddhism expanded its geographical range, and was established in places outside India – Sri Lanka being the first – they resorted to using Pali just as the brahmins used Sanskrit. After that, as mentioned in Chapter 1, the Pali tradition acquired a special word for commentary, *attha-kathā*, which literally means 'telling the meaning'.

To translate *attha-kathā* as 'telling the meaning' is not wrong, but misses an important ambiguity which has been widely overlooked. We say that a word or sentence has sound and meaning, and such a pairing is commonly referred to in both Sanskrit and Pali, but the two languages do so in different ways. Why?

'Sound' is *śabda* in Sanskrit, *sadda* in Pali, and dictionaries give the commonest English meanings as 'sound' and 'word'. The other half of the pair is more complicated. In Sanskrit it is *artha*, in Pali *aṭṭha* or *attha* (whether the double *t* is dental or cerebral is not relevant to the meaning and in this context is a red herring). This word has several meanings; two of the commonest are 'meaning' and 'purpose, intention'. It is never paired with *sadda* in Pāli, but with *vyañjana*. Though the *Pali-English Dictionary* gives this as 'letter (of a word)' – obviously because of its common pairing – its basic meaning is 'manifestation'. This shows that the underlying idea is that the words used manifest the intention of the speaker. So what language reveals, according to Pali, is not some metaphysical reality, but what speakers intend to convey.

The pragmatics ...

The *Araṇavibhaṅga Sutta* shows that the Buddha's attitude to language was pragmatic: his purpose was to convey meaning, and anything that might impede communication was to be discarded. This is exactly what we would expect of the Buddha's famous 'skill in means'.

Thus the world came to see that, in contrast to the brahmins, the Buddhists had no problem with translating their message into other languages. There are other reasons too why brahminism and Buddhism have followed such very different courses through world history, but the mere fact that the brahmins held that their texts could not be translated from the original Sanskrit whereas the Buddhists favoured translation wherever it served the cause of proselytization would alone account for much of what happened down the centuries.

... and the metaphysics of language

This willingness to translate their teachings into any language had a momentous effect on Buddhist, and indeed world, history. For the brahmins, each Sanskrit word[47] is a kind of unchanging monolith, expressing its meaning throughout eternity and corresponding to a real entity, whether that entity happens to be manifest or not. There is a one-to-one correspondence between word and meaning, and meaning is always reference.

For the Buddha such a correspondence was unthinkable. He may have drawn this conclusion because he was aware that there were countries beyond India where Sanskrit was unknown and it was not plausible to argue (as the brahmins did) that their languages were just debased derivatives from it. But by whatever means he attained his insight, what matters most is that he knew that there is no one-to-one correspondence between language and reality.

I quoted from Sheldon Pollock above: '"All mental formations" (*sarve saṃskārāḥ, sabbe saṃkhārā*) – in fact, all things formed, no doubt including all Vedic rites (*saṃskāra*) and perhaps even Sanskrit itself (*saṃskṛta*) "are non-eternal"; they arise, and having arisen, disappear.' In order fully to understand the Buddhist nature of Pali, we need to unpack this further.

For the Buddha, there are no unchanging entities, only processes. All our apperceptions (*saññā*) are empty (*suñña*),[48] which means that nothing in them is unchanging. This lack of an unchanging essence is true of everything, not just the living individual: it is the generalisation to all phenomena of the principle of having 'no soul'. In the same text the Buddha says that every apperception is *saṃkhata*: constructed, the result of a process, and therefore impermanent and unsatisfactory (*dukkha*). Note that what is being said is that these qualities apply both to the act of apperception, the naming process, the use of language, and to what is being apperceived.

To put this in language more familiar to us: the Buddha concluded not merely that languages were conventional, but that it was inherently impossible for any language fully to capture reality. We can only express our cognition through language, using *saññā*, but that imposes on experience linguistic categories which cannot do justice to its fluidity – whether we consider experience subjectively, or prefer to think of it in objective terms as 'the world as experienced'.

This has been admirably expressed by Noa Ronkin:

> The Buddha ... unveils not only the dominance of language and conceptual thought, but also their inherent ... inadequacy. Although language is a constant feature of our experience, we are normally unaware of the paradox in the cognitive process: to become knowable all the incoming sensory data must be verbally differentiated, but as such they are mere constructions, mental formations; nothing justifies their reliability because they could equally have been constructed otherwise, in accordance with other conventional guidelines. ... He points towards conventionalism in language and underlines the misleading character of nouns as substance-words. What we can know is part of the activity of language, but language, by its very nature, undermines certified knowledge.[49]

The same would apply to any scripture in any language, but I think that the use of Pali neatly symbolises this position.

To move back to applying this argument at a

day-to-day level, I would like to record that the Ven. Dr Walpola Rahula once told me that everything the Buddha said could be expressed in any language. In the context, his claim was that he could and did teach in the West using only English without needing to use any Pali or Sanskrit words; but he also meant that this claim could be generalised and was an important facet of the Buddhist tradition. I often have occasion to wish that more people who try to present Buddhism in the West would demystify their offerings by purging them of foreign words.

The spirit not the letter

Pali also reflects the spirit of the Buddha's teaching in another way. It is consistent with his view of language that the Buddha shows a keen awareness of the dangers of literalism. He classifies people who listen to his teaching into four types. The first type understands the teaching as soon as it is uttered; the second understands on mature reflection; the third is educable: he can understand it when he has worked at it, thought about it, and cultivated wise friends. The fourth is called *pada-parama*, 'putting the words first': though he hears much, preaches much, remembers much and recites much he does not come to understand the teaching within this lifetime.[50]

A particularly famous text on the dangers of literalism is the *Alagaddūpama Sutta*,[51] which I have cited at some length in Chapter 3 when exemplifying repetition. The title of the text refers to the Buddha's simile: that a teaching is like a water snake.[52] If you grasp it at the back of the head, you can keep hold of it and use it as you please, but if you do not apply that technique it will probably kill you.

The occasion for this simile is that the monk Ariṭṭha claims that the Buddha has said that there is nothing wrong with a monk's having sexual intercourse. His argument exploits the ambiguity of the word *kāma*, which (like English 'desire') can have the narrow meaning of sexual desire or pleasure, or a far wider range of meaning. The Buddha reprimands him by saying that some people learn his teachings not for their meaning but because they want to shine in controversy and win debates. This is to grasp a teaching but to grasp it wrongly, so that it will only do you harm, as happens when you grasp a snake at a point on its body which allows it to turn and bite you.

After employing this simile, the Buddha then takes his line of argument further, using the famous simile of the raft. When one needs to cross a body of water one may cobble together a raft, but once that raft has served its purpose one leaves it behind. He concludes this comparison by saying, 'If you understand that they are like a raft, you should leave even my teachings behind, let alone things I have never taught.'

The last words, taken in context, refer to Ariṭṭha's misrepresentation of what the Buddha has said. Perhaps because they have not considered the context in which the Buddha is speaking, many readers and hearers of this final passage have misunderstood it in various ways. I have discussed this fascinating mistake and some of its consequences in a previous publication. Here I need only repeat:

> The point is not that the content of his teaching is to be abandoned once one is Enlightened, but that his teaching is pragmatic, a means to an end, and that one should not cling to a particular formulation he used – let alone to something he never said at all.[53]

To put it as simply as possible, the Buddha is saying: 'Don't try to take me literally: follow the spirit, not the letter.' It is truly ironic that people have failed to do as he urged, precisely by taking his words too literally.

I suggest that we can take the use of Pali to symbolise this cornerstone of the Buddha's teaching, an instruction or meta-teaching which I think may be unique to him.

No less important is the Buddha's explicit

statement: 'I have expressed my teaching in various ways': *pariyāya-desito mayā dhammo.* Two of the Buddha's followers are arguing over whether he has taught that there are two kinds of feeling (*vedanā*) or three. They appeal to his judgment. He says that he has presented the matter from different perspectives, so that at various times he has declared the number of feelings to be two, three, five, six, eighteen, thirty-six and a hundred and eight – to fit the context.[54] As Yakpitigedara Karunadasa has written:

> The clear message conveyed here is that what accords with actuality and, therefore, what is true need not be repeated in the same way as a holy hymn or a sacred mantra. Rather, what is true can be restated in many ways, from many different perspectives. As elsewhere, here too Buddhism avoids absolutism and dogmatism: there is no one absolutist way of presenting the Dhamma that must be dogmatically adhered to ... [T]he Buddha goes on to say that when the Dhamma has thus been presented in many different ways, one should not tenaciously adhere to one particular presentation, then argue and quarrel with others who base themselves on other presentations.[55]

This should of course apply not just to the Buddha

but to every teacher, including Buddhologists. I deeply regret that I have so far failed to use this quotation in my own accounts of the Dhamma.

Once we understand how the Buddha warned us against taking doctrines too literally, I think we can gain further insights into the nature of Buddhism. Why is the Canon presented to us in three parts? The *Vinaya* tells us what to do if we are serious about trying to attain Enlightenment; the other two parts tell us what we need to understand about ourselves and the world, but take contrasting approaches. The *Sutta Piṭaka* tells it in many ways, some of them, such as similes and metaphors, indirect; the *Abhidhamma Piṭaka* (which was composed not by the Buddha but by his followers) tells it literally. (Technically, the *Sutta Piṭaka* is said to employ 'ways round' (*sa-pariyāya*), whereas the *Abhidhamma* is free of them (*nippariyāya*).) This is comparable to the distinction between poetry and prose – but, reader, please beware of taking me literally!

The spirit in which the Buddha wished his teaching to be taken can be found in many parts of the Buddhist world. Let me conclude this brief survey with two contemporary examples: lay Buddhist villagers in Sri Lanka, and Buddhist nuns in Taiwan and mainland China.

When I did fieldwork in a Sinhalese village in central

Sri Lanka I was curious to find out exactly what the villagers made of the 'Five Precepts' which probably all of them knew by heart and many of them recited every day. The precepts are in Pali, a language which none of the villagers had studied, and although it is related to Sinhala, it is not similar enough to be easily intelligible to a Sinhala speaker. On making inquiries, I found out that although most people could not isolate all the Pali words and say what they meant, more or less everyone except very young children understood exactly what they were undertaking when they recited a precept. Perhaps even more important, many people spontaneously said that detailed understanding was not important. What counted was to make a conscious and sincere commitment to the whole: not to kill, not to steal, to avoid wrong sexual behaviour, not to lie, not to get drunk.

Details could be left to the monks to mull over. But villagers were well aware of the fundamental Buddhist principle that what matters is intention. Thus I doubt that anyone thought that not lying was to be taken literally: common courtesies such as compliments were not merely permitted but part of good behaviour; what was meant was not to try to deceive someone.

In Sri Lanka the five precepts are always taken *en bloc*. I have been told on good authority that in

Thailand a Buddhist may approach a monk and ask him to administer the precepts separately (*visuṃ visuṃ*). Thus, if he anticipates going to a boozy party where he intends to enjoy himself, he can ask not to take the fifth precept; if he is preparing for a business meeting at which he plans to make misleading claims or promises he can omit the fourth; and so on. This shows the strength of the tradition that a vow is not to be taken in bad faith.

Pragmatism

The Buddha's rejection of brahminical metaphysics and the use of Sanskrit can be seen as an aspect of his pragmatism. Let me cite some of the research findings of (Melody) Tzu-Lung Chiu in an article[56] based on her doctoral thesis for the University of Ghent. She conducted interviews in several nunneries in both Taiwan and mainland China to ask nuns about their observance of an attitude towards the monastic rules (*vinaya*) by which they had vowed to live. She found hardly any literalism or tendentious interpretation. On the contrary: most informants emphasised that one needs to understand the spirit and background of each precept while observing it, and no one suggested that knowledge of the background was irrelevant.

One typical teacher told her that one must protect and obey the precepts because each of them is an important aid towards achieving nirvana for oneself and other sentient beings. Anyone who was sincerely acting in the spirit of the precepts would not be disobeying them. Another said that the precepts are like civil laws: they are not intended to be restrictive, and if one feels constrained by them that is because of one's psychological attitude.

To be pragmatic one should also be adaptable. If one understood the historical origins of the precepts, one could make suitable adjustments to modern conditions. One nun even explicitly stated that scholars often made the mistake of reading *Vinaya* too literally and superficially, just examining the letter of the precepts. She used as an example the rule against nuns eating garlic: this had been laid down not because of the properties of garlic but because some nuns had once dug up all a layman's garlic, leaving none for him; monastics should be aware of and concerned about their lay supporters' economic conditions and not accept a gift which the donor could not afford.

Buddhist monks and nuns should not break local lay customs even though the Buddha did not lay down any rule specifically saying so. The nun took smoking as an example: many people smoke, but it is unsuitable for Buddhist monastics to do so. Lay custom also influences questions of monastic eating habits: Theravāda monks do not eat after midday, but on the other hand they eat meat without drawing criticism.

One can sum up in the words of the nun who told Dr Chiu that each monastery or organisation had its own viewpoint on the observance of the *vinaya* rules. There was no absolute right or wrong against which to judge the various ways of interpreting and practising rules; the way of observing the *vinaya* was pluralistic. The different attitudes and values that one can observe in regard to observing the precepts relate to differing conditions and contexts, educational backgrounds, religious practices, ways of propagating Buddhism both individually and institutionally, and levels of interaction with the laity, as well as the adaptability and flexibility of Buddhism more generally.

The study of Buddhism is difficult, because of its vast range in time and space and its being embedded in so many different environments. Differences in detail proliferate, and to learn about them demands expertise in many languages. Yet here, I would argue, we find Chinese nuns (all Mahāyānists) in the twenty-first century living their lives in what I see as the spirit exemplified by the ancient Buddhist use of Pali. Not only has the spirit survived: in doing so it has carried much of the letter along with it.

Epilogue

The Future of Pali

As I finish writing this book, two of my pupils, Alexander Wynne and Alex Wrona, are about to launch a major project in Pali pedagogy under the auspices of the Oxford Centre for Buddhist Studies (OCBS). Since this is the third instalment in my attempt to popularise the study of Pali, let me briefly explain the history of that endeavour.

From 1965 to 2004 I held positions at Oxford University to teach Sanskrit and Pali, with a strong emphasis on Sanskrit. When I took mandatory retirement on reaching the age of 67, I reflected on why I was dissatisfied with my record as a Pali teacher, despite having had students who were intelligent and gifted, and for the most part highly motivated. The level of their attainment at the end of a two-year course had been judged by a final written examination, tedious for examiner and examined alike.

I felt that several things had been less than ideal.

Let me summarise the three which I find the most important: (1) use of time; (2) learning inappropriately in terms of both goals and methods; (3) learning in isolation.

(1) By a tradition which would have been difficult to change, the Pali course lasted two years. The University had/has three terms a year, each lasting eight weeks, with two vacations of six weeks and a summer vacation of sixteen weeks. By the same tradition, Pali was taught throughout each term twice a week for one hour. So the Pali course consisted of sixteen contact hours per term, forty-eight hours per year, and ninety-six hours in all. Surely that should be enough to get a good grounding in the language?

The snag is the spacing. Half way through the course, there was a sixteen-week break, long enough to forget almost everything learnt so far. In theory, which generations ago may have had some remote connection to practice, students continued to study (mainly by themselves) during the vacations, but in those days social and economic conditions were very different, and in modern times almost all students find it necessary to take paid employment in the vacations. (Some take paid employment even in term time, even though many universities try to discourage this.)

It is clearly inefficient to study any subject with

so spaced out a timetable, and this is likely to apply powerfully to learning a language, the acquisition of which has to be cumulative, particularly in the early stages. Reforming this dysfunctional timetable is not possible so long as achievement is measured by a test on a specified day at the very end of the course.

(2) The goal of almost everyone who wants to learn Pali is – and should be – to read the teachings of the Buddha. Of course, most people begin by reading them in translation; but close study requires reading them in the original Pali. Often one learns a language because one wants to be able to speak it, understand it when spoken, write it and read it, but to Pali only the last applies, which means that it makes sense to leave aside several aspects – even if most people will want to know how to pronounce it. As for method, modern technology means that the traditional emphasis on memorisation is outmoded: dictionaries are even more accessible now that they have been digitised, and even grammatical forms can be assimilated by dint of meeting them constantly while reading, rather than spending time and effort on rote learning at the outset.

(3) Learning is enhanced if students work together. The present system, focussed on examinations, promotes competition, which is far less efficient than cooperation – partly because most people find

cooperation more enjoyable, but more importantly because many minds are better than one. It is possible to get members of a university Pali class to do some work together, but rarely outside term time.

There were other reasons why I found it necessary to write a new Pali course. For example, those available deal too little with syntax – Wilhelm Geiger's authoritative *Pali Grammar* has none at all! – and their account of the use of the dative is usually wrong. But this is not the place to explore these details.

I began my attempted improvements by holding residential courses for 12 days. The first ones were in Sharpham in Devon, later ones in Oxford. Residential courses were of course particularly successful in tackling problem (3) above, creating an *esprit de corps* among the students. Quite soon we added a significant improvement: Dr Tomoyuki Kono joined us as assistant teacher; he specialised in giving individual attention to the slower students, so that it became rare for anyone to be left behind.

The main drawback of the residential courses was financial: both students and teachers had to pay for board and lodging, and travel to the course venue was too costly for most overseas aspirants. In 2015 a pupil at an Oxford course, Ilona Budapesti, persuaded me to make a second attempt by giving the course live on-line, thus in effect opening it up to pupils all over the world; she also demonstrated how to do it, using Zoom. We experimented with different timings and formats, and more or less settled on a course given over 20 days, during which pupils were also expected to do some homework. There was teaching for about half the day on 18 days. I began each teaching day with a lecture, and then students were put into small groups to work together; there were one or two assistant teachers who visited the groups and helped both groups and individuals, as required. This variety of teaching provision was very effective.

We found, however, that there is no one perfect solution: take up of these courses soon became too patchy for them to be economically viable. For some, no doubt, they were too expensive, and probably others found it impractical to dedicate a block of three weeks to almost full time study.

It now seems that we should make a third attempt by offering courses which are easier to attend, because the timing is left to the pupil; they therefore have to be recorded rather than live. Thus they can also be considerably cheaper. Initially we lose all the ways we earlier devised for coping with problem (3), but in the course of time we may introduce such modifications as tutorials, for single pupils or groups. The material is based on the existent OCBS course book (which is copyright), but in the absence of live teaching that has to be heavily supplemented by further detail, and particularly by exercises. Both Wynne and Wrona, the creators of this course, have taught on the live on-line course and thus know the material well.

Each level of the online Pali course will include video instruction, online exercises, a vocabulary builder, and supplementary material including fact sheets, grammar tables and grammatical analyses of Pali teachings and texts. Details will be publicised on the OCBS webpage.

We welcome feedback, and hope that at last we may have hit on a way to spread an understanding of Pali much more widely throughout the world.

Notes

1 In this book I have decided to treat the word 'Pali', the name of a language, as an English word and therefore not to spell it with a diacritic 'Pāli', as a word within the language itself.

2 Originally published in German, 1936; English edition London, Yale University Press, 2005.

3 Burtt, E.A., *The Teachings of the Compassionate Buddha.* New York: New American Library, 1955.

4 Gombrich, Richard, *What the Buddha Thought*, Sheffield and Bristol, CT: Equinox, corrected edn 2013, p.1.

5 Norman, K.R., *Pali Literature*, Wiesbaden, Harrassowitz, 1983, pp.1–2.

6 Nikam, N.A. and McKeon, Richard (ed. and trans.), *The Edicts of Asoka.* Chicago: University of Chicago Press, 1959.

7 Norman, K.R., 'The dialects in which the Buddha preached', pp.61–77 in Heinz Bechert (ed.), *Die Sprache der ältesten buddhistischen Überlieferung: The Language of the Earliest Buddhist Tradition.* Göttingen, 1980.

8 Norman, *Pāli Literature*, p.2.

9 This has an alternative spelling: *aṭṭhakathā.*

10 Norman, K.R., 'The Origin of Pāli and its Position among the Indo-European Languages', *Journal of Pali and Buddhist Studies* (Nagoya) I, pp.1–27.

11 Hinüber, Oskar von, 'Notes on the Pali Tradition in Burma', *Nachrichten der Akademie der Wissenschaften in Göttingen. 1. Philologisch-historische Klasse*, nr. 3 (1983), pp.67–79.

12 Hinüber, Oskar von, 'The Oldest Pali Manuscript', Akademie der Wissenschaften und der Literatur, Mainz. *Abhandlungen der Geistes- und Sozialwissenschaftlichen Klasse*, nr. 6 (1991).

13 Hinüber, Oskar von, 'Epigraphical Varieties of Continental Pali from Devnimori and Ratnagiri', pp.185–200 in *Buddhism and Its Relation to Other Religions: Essays in Honour of Dr Shozen Kumoi on His Seventieth Birthday*, Kyoto 1985.
14 Norman, K.R., 'The Pali Language and Scriptures', pp.29–53 in T. Skorupski (ed.), *The Buddhist Heritage*. Tring, 1989.
15 Gombrich, Richard, 'Dating the Buddha: A Red Herring Revealed', pp.237–59 in Heinz Bechert (ed.), *The Dating of the Historical Buddha: Die Datierung des historischen Buddha, part 2*. Göttingen, 1992.
16 Hinüber, Oskar von, *Das Ältere Mittelindisch im Überblick*. Vienna, 1986, pp.22–23.
17 Pou, Saveros, 'Sanskrit, Pali and Khmero-Pali in Cambodia', pp.13–28 in J.G. de Casparis (ed.), *Sanskrit outside India, Panels of the VIIth World Sanskrit Conference* vols VI and VII (bound together). Leiden, 1991.
18 von Hinüber, 'Notes on the Pali Tradition in Burma', p.69.
19 Geiger, Wilhelm, trans. Batakrishna Ghosh, ed. K.R. Norman, *A Pāli Grammar*. Oxford, Pali Text Society, 1994.
20 Coulson, Michael, *Teach Yourself Sanskrit*. Hodder and Stoughton, *Teach Yourself Books*, London, 1st edn 1976. The book has since been through more than 20 editions.
21 Cone, Margaret and Richard F. Gombrich, *The Perfect Generosity of Prince Vessantara*. Oxford: Clarendon Press, 1977.
22 *Vinaya* I, 196 = *Udāna* V, 6.
23 *Sumaṅgala-vilāsinī* I, 22-3.
24 https://blogs.scientificamerican.com/observations/a-neuro-scientist-explores-the-sanskrit-effect/. Report by a graduate student on research by Dr James Hartzell of Basque Center on Cognition, Brain and Language (BCBL), Donostia, Spain, Center for Mind/Brain Sciences (CIMeC), University of Trento, Italy, and the Center for Buddhist Studies, Columbia University, USA, 11 January 2018.
25 *What the Buddha Thought*, p.102.
26 Perhaps 5th, more likely 4th century BCE.

27 Rhys Davids, T.W. and William Stede, *The Pali Text Society's Pali-English Dictionary* [1921–5]. Oxford, 1992.
28 Cone, Margaret, *A Dictionary of Pāli*. Oxford: Pali Text Society, 2001, etc.
29 In this section I use the translations published in *The Middle Length Discourses of the Buddha: a Translation of the Majjhima Nikāya* by Bhikkhu Ñāṇamoli and Bhikkhu Bodhi. Oxford: Pali Text Society, 1995.
30 *Majjhima Nikāya*, p.601.
31 *Majjhima Nikāya*, p.232. The lines of three dots function as ditto marks.
32 Bhikkhu Sujato and Bhikkhu Brahmali, *The Authenticity of the Early Buddhist Texts*. Oxford: Oxford Centre for Buddhist Studies, p.76 (free download).
33 Pollock, Sheldon, in *Axial Civilizations and World History*, pp.397–450, ed. Johann P. Arnason et al. Leiden: E.J. Brill, 2005. Originally presented as a paper to the Conference on Axial-Age Transformations, European University Institute, Florence, December, 2001.
34 I have substituted 'his' for Pollock's 'the'.
35 Pollock, p.406.
36 The Mīmāṃsakas were the theoreticians of Vedic ritual, particularly of sacrifice. [RG]
37 Pollock here gives a reference to my work. [RG]
38 Pollock, pp.408–9. Pollock's last point is only strengthened by the fact that he oversimplifies: the author is not always the Buddha: passages and even whole texts are sometimes ascribed to other speakers.
39 *Vinaya* II.139.
40 Gombrich, *What the Buddha Thought*, pp.146–8.
41 *Majjhima Nikāya sutta* 139.
42 For a complex and utterly convincing example, see Anālayo, *The Foundation History of the Nuns' Order, Hamburg Buddhist Studies* 6. Bochum/Freiburg: Numata Center for Buddhist Studies, 2016.
43 In a personal communication, Dr Imre Bangha says that he finds

a parallel in pre-modern New Indo-Aryan languages and offers examples from Brajbhasha.

44 Wikipedia article 'Shravasti'.

45 Rhys Davids, T., *Buddhist India*. New York: G.P. Putnam's Sons, 1903.

46 Definition by the dictionary on Google.

47 To be more precise, for inflecting words I should say root or stem.

48 *Cūla-suññatā sutta, Majjhima Nikāya sutta* 121.

49 Noa Ronkin, *Early Buddhist Metaphysics*. London and New York: RoutledgeCurzon, p.245.

50 *Aṅguttara Nikāya* II.135.

51 *Majjhima Nikāya sutta* 22.

52 In fact no one is quite sure what an *alagadda* is, but there seems to be a consensus that water snake fits the context.

53 *How Buddhism Began*, London and Atlantic Highlands NJ: Athlone, 1996, p.24.

54 *Bahuvedanīya sutta*, MN 1, 398.

55 Y. Karunadasa, *Early Buddhist Teachings*. Hong Kong, Centre of Buddhist Studies, University of Hong Kong, 2013, p.3.

56 Chiu, Tzu-Ling, 'An Overview of Buddhist Precepts in Taiwan and Mainland China,' *Journal of the Oxford Centre for Buddhist Studies*, 13 (2017), pp.151–97.

About the Author

Richard Gombrich is Chair and founding Director of the Oxford Centre for Buddhist Studies. From 1976 to 2004 he was Boden Professor of Sanskrit at the University of Oxford. He has been President of the Pali Text Society (1994–2002) and General Editor of the Clay Sanskrit Library.

Son of the eminent historian Ernst Gombrich, he studied at St Paul's School in London before entering Magdalen College, Oxford, in 1957, with a scholarship in classics (Greek and Latin). He received his BA in Oriental Studies in 1961, his DPhil in 1970, and an AM in Sanskrit from Harvard in 1963.

The author of numerous articles and books, including *How Buddhism Began* (1996) and *What The Buddha Thought* (2013), Richard is a leading authority on early Buddhism, and credited, among many other distinctions, with working out the dates of the Buddha's life and death.

Mud Pie Slices

Fresh Angles on Buddhism

Up Next …

Buddhism AND • Gay Watson

Buddhism and the Menopause • Claire O'Brien

Buddhism and Football • George Myerson

Buddhism and Walking • Tony Morris

Buddhism and God • Robert M. Ellis

Buddhism and Myth • Vishvapani Blomfield

Buddhism and the Brain • Wendy Lowes

Printed in Great Britain
by Amazon

81448550R00068